THE RAINBOW *Comes and Goes*

THE RAINBOW
Comes and Goes

A Mother and Son on
Life, *Love*, and *Loss*

ANDERSON COOPER AND
GLORIA VANDERBILT

HARPER

An Imprint of HarperCollins*Publishers*

HarperCollins books may be purchased for educational, business, or sales promotional use. For information, please e-mail the Special Markets Department at SPsales@harpercollins.com.

An extension of this copyright appears on page 291.

FIRST EDITION

Designed by Leah Carlson-Stanisic

Library of Congress Cataloging-in-Publication Data

Names: Cooper, Anderson. | Vanderbilt, Gloria, 1924- author.
Title: The rainbow comes and goes : a mother and son on life, love, and loss / Anderson Cooper and Gloria Vanderbilt.
Description: First edition. | New York : HarperCollins Publishers, 2016.
Identifiers: LCCN 2016000369| ISBN 9780062454942 (hardback) | ISBN 9780062454966 (ebook) | ISBN 9780062466730 (large print)
Subjects: LCSH: Cooper, Anderson. | Cooper, Anderson—Correspondence. | Television journalists—United States—Biography. | Vanderbilt, Gloria, 1924– | Vanderbilt, Gloria, 1924– Correspondence. | Celebrities—United States—Biography. | Mothers and sons—United States—Correspondence. | BISAC: BIOGRAPHY & AUTOBIOGRAPHY / Editors, Journalists, Publishers. | FAMILY & RELATIONSHIPS / General.
Classification: LCC PN4874.C683 A3 2016 | DDC 070.92—dc23 LC record available at http://lccn.loc.gov/2016000369

ISBN: 978-0-06-245494-2
ISBN: 978-0-06-247265-6 (B&N signed edition)
ISBN: 978-0-06-249185-5 (BAM signed edition)

16 17 18 19 20 OV/RRD 10 9 8 7

THE RAINBOW *Comes and Goes*

Introduction

My mother comes from a vanished world, a place and a time that no longer exist. I have always thought of her as a visitor stranded here; an emissary from a distant star that burned out long ago.

Her name is Gloria Vanderbilt. When I was younger I used to try to hide that fact, not because I was ashamed of her—far from it—but because I wanted people to get to know me before they learned that I was her son.

Vanderbilt is a big name to carry, and I've always been glad I didn't have to. I like being a Cooper. It's less cumbersome, less likely to produce an awkward pause in the conversation when I'm introduced. Let's face it, the name Vanderbilt has history, baggage. Even if you don't know the details of my

mom's extraordinary story, her name comes with a whole set of expectations and assumptions about what she must be like. The reality of her life, however, is not what you'd imagine.

My mom has been famous for longer than just about anyone else alive today. Her birth made headlines, and for better or worse, she's been in the public eye ever since. Her successes and failures have played out on a very brightly lit stage, and she has lived many different lives; she has been an actress, an artist, a designer, and a writer; she's made fortunes, lost them, and made them back again. She has survived abuse, the loss of her parents, the death of a spouse, the suicide of a son, and countless other traumas and betrayals that might have defeated someone without her relentless determination.

Though she is a survivor, she has none of the toughness that word usually carries with it. She is the strongest person I know, but tough, she is not. She has never allowed herself to develop a protective layer of thick skin. She's chosen to remain vulnerable, open to new experiences and possibilities, and because of that, she is the most youthful person I know.

My mom is now ninety-two, but she has never looked her age and she has rarely felt it, either. People often say about someone that age, "She's as sharp as ever," but my mom is actually *sharper* than ever. She sees her past in perspective.

The little things that once seemed important to her no longer are. She has clarity about her life that I am only beginning to have about mine.

At the beginning of 2015, several weeks before her ninety-first birthday, my mother developed a respiratory infection she couldn't get rid of, and she became seriously ill for the first time in her life. She didn't tell me how bad she felt, but as I was boarding a plane to cover a story overseas, I called her to let her know I was leaving, waiting until the last minute as usual because I never want her to worry. When she picked up the phone, immediately I knew something was wrong. Her breath was short, and she could barely speak.

I wish I could tell you I canceled my trip and rushed to her side, but I didn't. I'm not sure if the idea she could be very ill even occurred to me; or perhaps it did, acting on it would have been just too inconvenient and I didn't want to think about it. I was heading off on an assignment, and my team was already in the air. It was too late to back out.

Shortly after I left, she was rushed to the hospital, though I didn't find this out until I had returned, and by then she was already back home.

For months afterward she was plagued with asthma and a continued respiratory infection. At times she was unsteady on her feet. The loss of agility was difficult for her, and there were many days when she didn't get out of bed. Several of her close friends had recently died, and she was feeling her age for the first time.

"I'd like to have several more years left," she told me. "There are still things I'd like to create, and I'm very curious to see how it all turns out. What's going to happen next?"

As her ninety-first birthday neared, I began to think about our relationship: the way it was when I was a child and how it was now. I started to wonder if we were as close as we could be.

The deaths of my father and brother had left us alone with each other, and we navigated the losses as best we could, each in our own way. My father died in 1978, when I was ten; and my brother, Carter, killed himself in 1988, when I was twenty-one, so my mom is the last person left from my immediate family, the last person alive who was close to me when I was a child.

We have never had what would be described as a conventional relationship. My mom wasn't the kind of parent you would go to for practical advice about school or work. What she does know about are hard-earned truths, the kind of things you discover only by living an epic life filled with love and loss, tragedies and triumphs, big dreams and deep heartaches.

When I was growing up, though, my mom rarely talked about her life. Her past was always something of a mystery. Her parents and grandparents died before I was born, and I knew little about the tumultuous events of her childhood, or of the years before she met my father, the events that shaped the person she had become. Even as an adult, I found there was still much I didn't know about her—experiences she'd had, lessons she'd learned that she hadn't passed on. In many cases, it was because I hadn't asked. There was also much she didn't know about me. When we're young we all waste so much time being reserved or embarrassed with our parents, resenting them or wishing they and we were entirely different people.

This changes when we become adults, but we don't often explore new ways of talking and conversing, and we put off discussing complex issues or raising difficult questions. We think we'll do it one day, in the future, but life gets in the way, and then it's too late.

I didn't want there to be anything left unsaid between my mother and me, so on her ninety-first birthday I decided to start a new kind of conversation with her, a conversation about her life. Not the mundane details, but the things that really matter, her experiences that I didn't know about or fully understand.

We started the conversation through e-mail and continued it for most of the following year. My mom had only started to use e-mail recently. At first her notes were one or two lines long, but as she became more comfortable typing, she began sending me very detailed ones. As you will see in the pages ahead, her memories are remarkably intimate and deeply personal, revealing things to me she never said face-to-face.

The first e-mail she sent me was on the morning of her birthday.

91 years ago on this day, I was born.

I recall a note from my Aunt Gertrude, received on a birthday long ago.

"Just think, today you are 17 whole years old!" she wrote.

Well, today—I am 91 whole years old—a hell of a lot wiser, but somewhere still 17.

What is the answer?

What is the secret?

Is there one?

That e-mail and its three questions started the conversation that ended up changing our relationship, bringing us closer than either of us had ever thought possible.

It's the kind of conversation I think many parents and their grown children would like to have, and it has made this past year the most valuable of my life. By breaking down the walls of silence that existed between us, I have come to understand my mom and myself in ways I never imagined.

I know now that it's never too late to change the relationship you have with someone important in your life: a parent, a child, a lover, a friend. All it takes is a willingness to be honest and to shed your old skin, to let go of the long-standing assumptions and slights you still cling to.

I hope what follows will encourage you to think about your own relationships and perhaps help you start a new kind of conversation with someone you love.

After all, if not now, when?

One

A flashback this morning when I woke up: it's my seventeenth birthday and I'm striding along Madison Avenue, hastening to meet my boyfriend.

I *knew* the excitement, the anticipation that girl felt, and in knowing, I became, for an instant, seventeen once again.

But I am not seventeen. I am ninety-one.

No longer can I stride or hasten. I was unaware that if I lived long enough, there would come a time when this would be impossible. When I was seventeen this never crossed my mind; nor did it as the years passed and I got older. I was aware that "old age" happened, but to other people, not to me. Perhaps it's because, as a child, I did not have parents and siblings as most people do, and I didn't experience the circling spans of life and death.

My first reaction upon reaching ninety-one is surprise. How did it happen so quickly? Am I ready for it?

If I am ninety-one, it means my time on this earth is racing to the finish line. Will I have the power to complete the race with a badge of courage, leaving those I love with a memory of me that will sustain them and give them strength when I am gone?

Until I fell ill with influenza and asthma this year, I believed my best years were ahead. I'd been blessed with superb health all my life, so it was a shock to find myself suddenly on a stretcher in an ambulance, the sirens leading me to New York Hospital, where your father, Wyatt Cooper, was taken by ambulance thirty-seven years ago, the hospital where he died.

Asthma is a terrifying experience, like having a tourniquet strangling your throat. You choke, gasp for air, wonder, "Is this it? Is this how I will die? Please, God, or whoever you are—*not yet.*" It is a cliché, but a true one, and I understand it only now: Health is your most treasured gift. As long as you have it, you are independent, master of yourself. Illness grabs the soul. You plunge in and out of hope, fearing you will never recover. All that I have been, all that I am, all that I might become no longer exist. I am alone. Nothing can distract from the truth of this finality.

How can my body betray me when there is so much still to be done? You see, it isn't age itself that betrays you; it is your body, and with its deterioration goes your power. You end up obsessed, entirely focused on your health, paying attention to every nuance, every ache and pain. Instead of working or living your life, you waste your time on appointments with doctors.

Do you know the poem by Algernon Charles Swinburne?

From too much love of living,
From hope and fear set free,
We thank with brief thanksgiving
Whatever Gods may be
That no life lives for ever;
That dead men rise up never;
That even the weariest river
Winds somewhere safe to sea.

It is no mystery where time is leading us. No secret the road we are on. Hand in hand, or fist to fist, we move forward at a snail's pace, relentlessly bent in one direction, toward the same end.

Death.

The word leaves a smear across the page as I write it in my journal. There is no denial, no wriggling out of it. The more I try to erase it, the deeper it grinds into a smudge of black blood. There is no other truth to depend on, no other certainty. It is as inevitable as birth. Death is the price we pay for being born.

How we die is another matter. If terminally ill, we have the choice to take our own life. Secretly somewhere inside me lies the notion that I will slip away quietly in my sleep.

There is also the vague, crazy fantasy or hope that it simply is not going to happen to me. Perhaps I inherited this indomitable optimism from my mother's mother, Laura Delphine Kilpatrick Morgan, whom I called Naney. She stipulated in her will that two nuns sit by her open coffin in rotating shifts for the four days leading up to her burial, to ensure that her eyes did not suddenly open and that she was actually dead.

Ready or not, I know that someday there really will be no more "you," no more "me." And when it happens, we will be hurled into infinity with no chance of return.

But don't worry. I am on the mend. Last night I dreamt I jumped over that dwarf planet Pluto, trillions of miles away, the one they have sent a spacecraft to get pictures of for the first time. It was a cinch.

Your Naney Morgan had nuns sit by her coffin for four days to make sure she really was dead? I didn't realize you could get nuns to do that.

I can't imagine what it's like to be ninety-one. I'm still adjusting to the idea of turning forty-eight, which I will in a few months. I haven't told you this before, but I've always assumed I would die at fifty because that is how old Daddy was when he died.

My doctor has assured me repeatedly I will live well past that, but I don't entirely believe him. The benefit of thinking you will die at fifty is that it can spur you to accomplish a lot of things at a young age, which is what I have attempted to do, but now the prospect of living longer makes me uncertain about the plans I've made.

Clearly, I have not inherited your Naney Morgan's spirit of optimism. I know that, as a child, you were very close to her, but other than that I don't really know anything about her.

I've always wondered why, when we were growing up, you didn't talk about your past. By the time I was six or seven, Carter and I knew all about Daddy's childhood on a farm in Quitman, Mississippi. He frequently recounted stories about his brothers and sisters and their large extended family. He told us about his troubled relationship with his father and his deep connection to the place where he was born, but you never mentioned your family. Did you just find it too difficult to bring up?

It never ever occurred to me to talk to you or Carter about my childhood. My life had been scrambled, so filled with strange events and surreal subplots, that to try to lay them out would have been like combining Franz Kafka's *The Trial* with Thornton Wilder's *Our Town*.

Also, your father didn't have just anecdotes to tell you about his childhood—he was a great photographer and had hundreds of pictures to illustrate whom and what he was talking about. The people in these photographs gazed into the camera, free of makeup and artifice. I couldn't help but wonder what they would think of me if they had any idea of the chaos I had come from.

Of course, I spoke to your father about what happened to me, but trying to explain my feelings exhausted me, and all that emerged was a brief encapsulation, nothing that got to the heart of the matter.

If it was too complicated to lay it out for the man I loved, how could I even begin to translate it for my children?

I had never had the experience of talking about my thoughts and feelings. When I was a child, adults really didn't communicate very much with children. I needed time to sort out what had happened, to understand the motivations of others that I had not been aware of as a child.

The first time I went to a psychiatrist, I was about twenty-seven. I sat down in his office, and said, "I'm here, but there's one thing I don't want to talk about: my mother."

Well, that was ridiculous of course; it was exactly what I did want to talk about, as I was still fearful of my mother in many ways. It is one of the blessings of age that the fear is now gone.

I later had an extraordinary experience with a different therapist. In 1960, LSD was being heralded as a possibly miraculous new way for some patients to delve into unexplored areas of the subconscious. My therapist asked if I wanted to try it under his supervision, and I eagerly said yes.

Even today, I can recall everything that happened in that one session as if it were a few hours ago.

I saw myself as an infant in 1925, in my crib at my father's house in Newport, while he lay in the next room dying. I heard footsteps running through the hallways, doors opening and closing, voices signaling to each other. It was night, and I knew something terrible was happening. I could stop it, I believed, if only I could get out of my crib and go to my father, but I lay on my back in the darkness, fists clenched, unable to do anything.

Suddenly the noises stopped. The door to my room opened. Sharp against the light from the hall was the shadow of my beloved governess, Dodo, and my father's mother, my Grandmother Vanderbilt. They drew close together as they stood whispering to each other in the silence. Screaming, I pulled myself up against the bars of the crib, still believing that if I could get to my father I could save him. Dodo picked me up and rocked me in her arms, while Grandma patted me, but I kept screaming. Yet they didn't take me to him. I choked on my tears, unable to tell them anything at all.

What I experienced while using LSD changed my life. It enabled me to reconcile with my mother after fifteen years of estrangement and begin to put together the pieces of the puzzle of my past.

———

Before you read any further, I should probably fill you in a little on my mother's background, so you can better understand some of the events she is referring to. Much of it is new to me as well, and I had to look it up in history books, since she had never mentioned it.

My mother was born Gloria Laura Vanderbilt in 1924, into a family of tremendous wealth. The first Vanderbilt to arrive in America was named Jan Aertson. He came to the Dutch settlement of New Amsterdam in 1650 as an indentured servant hoping to escape a life of poverty in Europe. He settled on Staten Island, and that is where his descendants remained for nearly a century, until Jan Aertson's great-great-great-grandson Cornelius Vanderbilt changed the family's fortunes forever.

Cornelius dropped out of school when he was eleven and began working on his father's boat ferrying passengers and cargo between Staten Island and Manhattan. By sixteen, he was in business for himself, using a small two-masted schooner in the waters around Manhattan. Cornelius was a cunning businessman and eventually moved into the steamship business.

He was frugal and restless, and expanded his empire by buying real estate and, later, railroad lines, which he combined to create the New York Central Railroad. When he died in 1877, he had amassed one of the greatest fortunes of his time, worth more than one hundred million dollars, which today would be equal to about two billion.

My mother's father, Reginald Claypoole Vanderbilt, was Cornelius's great-great-grandson. When he turned twenty-one he inherited millions of dollars from a family trust, but Reginald had none of Cornelius's work ethic. Reginald liked horses, gambling, and drinking. He died in 1925 of cirrhosis of the liver. He was just forty-five, and my mother was fifteen months old.

My grandmother Gloria Morgan was Reginald's second wife, having married him two years before his death. She was eighteen when she gave birth to my mom, and was completely unprepared to be a widow or a parent.

Like many children born into wealthy families at that time, my mother was taken care of by a governess. Her name was Emma Keislich, but my mother called her "Dodo." She was the most important person in my mother's young life.

ANDERSON COOPER and
Gloria Vanderbilt

"YOU DON'T GROW UP MISSING WHAT YOU NEVER HAD,
BUT THROUGHOUT LIFE THERE IS HOVERING OVER YOU
AN INESCAPABLE LONGING FOR SOMETHING YOU NEVER
HAD."

—*Susan Sontag*

As a child, you generally aren't aware that
your family is different from any other. You have no frame of
reference. It is only later that you learn your upbringing was
not the same as everybody else's.

My father died when I was fifteen months old. I have no
memory of him, and never missed him until I came to know
that it was unusual for a child not to have a father. He remains,
as he always has been, a photograph in a picture frame. Growing up, I was passionately curious about him, but no one except Dodo ever mentioned his name.

She told me he was "a darling," and that he loved horses.
But that was about it. Did he love me? I never dared ask, and
she never said.

Later, in my twenties, she handed me a sapphire ring, claiming that my father had given it to her when I was an infant with
the instructions "Keep it and give it to Gloria when she grows
up, because she's going to like jewelry."

Well, he was right about that.

I was thrilled. It was a message from him. A long-awaited sign that he did love me. But the story seemed odd, unlikely somehow. When I finally took the ring to be insured, I was told it was not a real sapphire.

My father was an alcoholic. Perhaps, in an expansive moment, inspired by the sentimental impulse of a cloudy fantasy, he had reached out to Dodo and given her the ring. But if so, where had it come from?

I said nothing to Dodo. The ring may have been from my father, but it also may have been a kindly gesture on her part, a way to prove that I once had a father who cared about me.

When your father and I were living in the house on Sixty-Seventh Street, shortly after you were born, we were robbed, and the ring was stolen along with the rest of my jewelry. I never saw it again.

Y ou used to quote a writer, Mary Gordon, who said, "A fatherless girl thinks all things possible and nothing safe."

For a long time I didn't understand what that meant or how it related to you. Now I do understand, and I think it's true of fatherless boys as well. I certainly think it applies to me.

When you lose a parent at an early age, you lose the fantasy of childhood. The veil is lifted. You learn that bad things happen and that no amount of crying or hugging will make them all right. Nothing is safe, and all things are possible: good things, beautiful things, but ugly and harmful things, too.

We both learned this lesson in different ways when we were ten years old: you with the custody case that thrust you into the headlines. and me with my father's death. The person I was and   e very different from the per   change I think you experien   l.

After my f   yself, and when I emerged, I   and serious. I'd become an ol   nstead of a participant in it. Nothing has ever felt safe since.

"I suspect that being fatherless leaves a woman with a taste for the fanatical, having grown unsheltered, having never seen in the familiar flesh the embodiment of the ancient image of authority, a fatherless girl can be satisfied only with the heroic, the desperate, the extreme. A fatherless girl thinks all things possible and nothing safe."

That is the full quote from Mary Gordon's novel *The Company of Women*, and when I came across it, I knew it to be the foundation of my life. It explained countless actions I'd taken thoughtlessly. Unbeknownst to me, my life decisions had been based on this principle. Even now that my eyes have been opened, they still are.

For a long time I couldn't identify the impact of my father's absence; it's taken me years to see it, but now it is all so clear. Looking back, I see time and time again that decisions I made, impulses I followed, and the kind of men I was attracted to all stemmed from my not having a father.

I used to imagine that my father had left me a letter, or a series of letters that would be delivered at key junctures of my life. I still hold out hope that one will show up.

It's interesting that you fantasized that he had written you a letter. For a long time I have had the same fantasy, that I would receive a letter from my dad. It may sound silly, but I still think about it every time I see a stack of mail waiting for me to go through, and it always makes me sad.

I hold on to the hope that there is a note from him somewhere out there that will reveal all the things I want to know about him, all the things I wish he'd had time to tell me.

Several months ago, I sent you a copy of a public radio interview he gave in 1976. It had been restored and posted online by Clocktower Radio.

It was so strange to sit in my office at work and suddenly hear his voice coming through the speaker on my desk. It was the first time I had heard it since I was ten years old. He didn't sound like I remembered, and I wouldn't have recognized his voice if I hadn't known it was him. He was talking about me and Carter and the close relationship he shared with us. I couldn't help but wonder what he would think of me now, and what it would be like to have a father still.

He was alive for only a fraction of my life, and yet there isn't a day that goes by that I don't think of him and miss him. The feelings of loss remain so sharp, and I still feel a twinge of anger toward him for dying, the irrational anger of a ten-year-old boy who suddenly learns that anything can happen and nothing is safe.

Although you lost your dad when you were so young, you did have him as the major influence in your life until you were ten. It's said that even though our brains do not fully develop until we are in our early twenties, the first seven years of our lives are crucial for influencing future development. Your dad gave you a firm base and a sense of the familial bonds he experienced from birth.

It was a gift I could never give you, as I didn't have this. I was not bound to any place or person. What I do have are little souvenirs of my past: my father's cigarette case, my mother's brush, and family photographs in frames. This is the only

ANDERSON COOPER and

Gloria Vanderbilt

evidence I have that I did in fact belong to a family, though I so often felt like an imposter.

I point these items out to you now when you come to visit because it is my way of telling you part of my history and because I often wish Dodo, Naney, and others had revealed more things to me in this way. Everyone's life is a story, and these things are part of the story—my story and your story, too, because you are my son.

As I write this, I can see a photograph of my father, this man I never knew, in a silver frame on my desk. I have more than once written him a letter and imagined I would stuff it in a bottle, seal it tight, then walk down a few blocks to the East River and twirl it fiercely around my head before hurling it into the rushing water.

OH DAD, POOR DAD, MAMMA'S HUNG YOU IN THE CLOSET AND
I'M FEELIN' SO SAD

—The title of a play by Arthur Kopit

Daddy,
How strange it feels to write that word. I am, after all, writing to a stranger. You departed when I was fifteen months old, not that you had anything to say about it—I'm well aware of that. Still, off you went, leaving only a photograph for me "to tell my troubles to," as Irving Berlin says in the song. What

ANDERSON COOPER and
Gloria Vanderbilt

*consolation is that? Your demeanor in the picture is that of a
stranger gingerly holding a porcelain infant, afraid it might
break.*

*Am I being unfair? No doubt, but that photograph is the
only tangible evidence I have to hang on to when I try to vent
my frustrations. I am angry that your absence almost from
my birth left me foundering this way and that, a ship without
rudder or sail, not knowing where to seek safety.*

*Whoever is reading this letter: You may take it for
granted, but not everyone is blessed with a dad—or a mom,
for that matter. Although I may sound pissed off at my father,
the truth of the matter is that I am crazy about the idea of
him and spent a lot of my time growing up fantasizing about
how much he would have loved me. Over the years, I have
tried to prove it by getting much older men to fall in love
with me.*

*Daddy, you were passionate about horses, and for a few
years I pretended I loved them too. That is, until I fell off a
horse while learning to jump and decided you would still love
me even if I stopped riding, which I did. What a relief, not to
pretend anymore. I gave up trying to please you. You were lost
to me. You weren't there and never would be.*

*I had to let you go, Daddy. Sad, so sad, I put you in the
closet, and I'm feeling so bad.*

I still have that picture of us on my dressing table. It doesn't upset me anymore, even though it's all I ever had and will have of you.

"The Dark Is Light Enough."

Your loving daughter, Gloria

———

Reginald Vanderbilt inherited millions of dollars from his family, but by the time he died he had spent nearly all of it. He was in debt, and there was little left for his young wife, my grandmother. A five-million-dollar trust fund had been set up for Reginald's offspring, however, and upon his death it was divided between Cathleen Vanderbilt (his twenty-one-year-old daughter from a previous marriage) and my fifteen-month-old mother, who would not receive her share until she turned twenty-one.

Because Gloria Morgan Vanderbilt, my grandmother, was not yet old enough to be legal guardian of my mother, New York Surrogate Court Judge James Foley was put in control of her trust fund. My grandmother was given a monthly stipend of four thousand dollars, and Surrogate Foley allowed her to move to Paris with her identical twin sister, Thelma; their mother, Nancy Morgan; my mother; and her governess, Dodo.

———

After my father died, my mother never mentioned him to me, and she never once spoke of the Vanderbilts. She hotfooted it out of Newport and took me and Dodo and Naney to Paris, where we lived along with my mother's identical twin sister, Thelma, on the Avenue Charles Floquet. We had a big house, and Dodo, Naney, and I were installed on a separate floor from my mother and Thelma.

My mother led an active social life, going every day to lunches, cocktail parties, dinners, and cabarets. Though Naney, Dodo, and I lived in the same house as she, it didn't feel like we did. It was as if two families were occupying one house. We had our floor, and a beautiful stranger glimpsed only fleetingly, my mother, occupied the rest.

Though I rarely saw her, I had Dodo and Naney, and I was happy. Dodo had been with me from the moment I was born. Cut by cesarean section from my mother's womb, I was handed straight into Dodo's arms. My newborn body took root in her embrace and found a home. Dodo's voice was the first I heard. Naney's the second. They were all the family I needed.

In my young eyes, they were a couple: Mother Dodo and Father Naney.

They were my parents, wrapping me with love as though with swaddling cloth, while my so-called real mother and father left for a ten-month European vacation soon after I was born. I was a baby, and they thought there was no point in spending time with me.

How to describe Dodo? Sometimes she was a mountain of soft sheep's wool for me to sink into; other times, a tree rooted so deep in earth that no thunder, wind, or rain, no storm of day or night, could rip my arms from her. In later years, it made me feel safe to just sit with her in a room without talking.

Naney offered me this sense of security as well, but in a much different way; incapable of holding back the extravagance of her affection, she demonstrated it by showering me with love, and chattering away. Her voice sounded like the tweeting of birds mingled with castanets.

It wasn't until we began to go for strolls in the Bois de Boulogne that I saw women and men walking together pushing baby carriages or playing games with children who called them "Mama" and "Papa" and whom they seemed to know very well indeed. That is how I learned what might have been for me if my father hadn't "gone to heaven," as Dodo once told me. But at the time I didn't feel deprived or that I was missing something. That came much later.

Your parents left you for ten months after you were born so they could go on a trip? That is incredible. I know, in those days, it was not unusual for wealthy parents to hand their kids over to a governess to raise, but it's hard to imagine that your mother was so completely uninterested in spending that time with you.

Did things change once you got a little older and you were in Paris with her? Did she start to take more of an interest in you?

During our first year in Europe, Aunt Thelma lived with us, and she and my mother were always out having fun. When I did see them, they were usually on their way out the door to a dinner or a party, and they looked so alike I couldn't tell one from the other.

They were knockout beautiful, and more than anything I wanted to be like them when I grew up! If I could be that beautiful, I believed, I would have power and everything would be all right. More than all right—it would be perfect. I longed to meld into my mother, but she was always out of reach.

The closest I came to her was when Marie, her maid, let me go up to the top floor, where she tended to my mother's clothes. There I found dresses in fabrics so soft to the touch. I remember spreading my palm to touch a dress made of buttery yellow velvet, as it hung in the closet. I have not since seen or been able to recapture that color in a painting, but it is clear as can be in my mind's eye. I held that dress against my face, taking a deep breath, the scent lingering from the flacon of Shalimar on my mother's dressing table consuming me. Longing to hug her, I tightened my hand into a fist around the soft fabric and pulled it to me.

"*Mais non! NON!* Miss Gloria, *sois gentille*," Marie called out, angry I might leave a mark on the velvet. All I ever wanted was for my mother to love me.

I didn't know you'd stayed so long in Europe as a child. For some reason I thought it was only for a year or two. Did your aunt Thelma live with you the whole time?

I lived in Europe until I was eight, but we traveled around a lot. Aunt Thelma married Lord Marmaduke Furness, a very rich British aristocrat, and she moved into his house in London and their country estate near Melton Mowbray.

While I don't have many memories of my mother, I do have flashbacks of Naney and Dodo in Paris, whispering in the bathroom with the light left on and the door partly open. I was afraid of the dark, so after they'd tucked me in, they would stay in the bathroom until I fell asleep. I'd lie in bed mesmerized by the soft sound of their hisses coming from within that slit of light. Gazing up at the ceiling, I'd catch occasional flashes of headlights from cars passing in the street below. I thought if I lay still, nothing bad could happen, so that's what I'd do, and eventually I'd drift off.

I've since realized this is when the plotting began. Naney, a master strategist, idolized Napoléon and always kept a copy of Emil Ludwig's biography of him by her bed. She'd underlined passages throughout the book that had special meaning to her. It's hard to know exactly when she came up with the plan, but soon it wasn't only at night that she and Dodo conspired—it continued on into the day, when they took me to play in the park.

They talked about a German prince named Friedel Hohenlohe, the great-grandson of Queen Victoria. He and my mother were in love, and she planned to marry him and take me to live in his castle in Germany. Naney hated Germans and wanted to figure out a way to stop the romance and get me away from my mother.

"She's an American girl and should be brought up in the United States with her American family," she kept saying.

Dodo also chattered constantly to me about "going to meet your family."

I didn't know what they were talking about. I had already met my family. Dodo and Naney were my family.

I wonder if your mom considered Dodo to be part of your family as you did. I imagine not. It is always interesting to me how children perceive things compared to adults.

When I think of our family for the first ten years of my life, I think of you, Daddy, Carter, and also May McLinden, the no-nonsense Scottish nanny who took care of me from the time I was born. She was quick to laugh and loved Carter and me as her own. She had no children, but she had us, and we had her.

Looking back, I realize I didn't know you all that well for the first ten years of my life. I was certainly closer to you than you'd been with your mother, but you worked a lot and were often traveling. The designer jeans you became so well known for hadn't come out yet, but when I was a child you were designing home furnishings and frequently traveled the country to make in-store appearances. I knew Stan and Chris, your sons from your previous marriage, to Leopold Stokowski, but they had already moved out of the house, and I don't recall much about them from that time.

I do remember a little about the house we lived in for the first six years of my life. It was a large limestone building on Sixty-Seventh Street, off Park Avenue, and perched on either side of the entrance were two imposing stone lions my father bought.

The town house still stands, but it's now an ambassador's residence. It saddens me to walk by it. The wisteria Daddy planted outside the entrance is still there and has taken over one side of the house. I think of him every time I see it.

There was a grand foyer with a black-and-white check marble floor and a curving staircase that went up the center of the building. I remember only some of the rooms, which you had meticulously decorated, and I recall you were constantly changing things: reupholstering furniture, repainting walls, moving pictures around.

You covered one bedroom entirely in patchwork quilts: the walls, the floor, the ceiling, even the furniture. Stepping inside it was like walking into a kaleidoscope.

The dining room walls were covered with antique Chinese wallpaper, and you frequently entertained actors and artists, directors and writers. Truman Capote, Lillian Gish, Gordon Parks, Charles Addams, and Liza Minnelli were among the guests, and even though Carter and I were very young, we were expected to sit at the table conversing with them. At the time, it didn't seem unusual to me, but it is so different from the way you were raised.

I remember the room I shared with Carter, on the top floor of the house, and just down the hall lived May. You've told me that when I was born Carter was less than thrilled by my arrival, though you had gone to great lengths to try to prepare him for the shock of no longer being the only child in the house. In most of the pictures from that time, I'm smiling smugly, while Carter chews the inside of his lip, annoyed at the indignity of having to pose with this plump interloper.

I was outgoing and funny. Carter was smarter, more serious and sensitive. As a child, he read voraciously and loved history and literature. I would follow him around, trying to imitate him as best I could, pretending to read the same books, agreeing with the opinions he so freely stated. Because Carter collected toy soldiers, so did I, and we would stage daylong war games on our bedroom floor: Crusaders battled Turks, Germans fought Americans, British colonial forces faced off against Zulus.

Even when you were home, I could always tell you felt slightly uncomfortable in the role of parent. I never doubted your love for me, but you carried with you a sadness, a slight distance you seemed to find hard to overcome. My father was such a presence in our lives, so comfortable being a parent, that I think it made you feel at times less than adequate. I didn't know then, of course, that you had never really had a mother or a father, or a stable family life.

That you were related to the Vanderbilt family had little significance for me. When I was about five or six, my father showed me the statue of Cornelius Vanderbilt that stands outside Grand Central Station in New York City, and it gave me the idea that all grandparents turned into statues when they died.

Later, when my class visited the Museum of Natural History, the teacher pointed to the statue of Teddy Roosevelt on the front steps and asked if anyone knew who it was.

I raised my hand. "I think it's my grandfather," I said.

I recall meeting a few cousins from your branch of the family, but I didn't understand how we were related, and I never had the sense that you felt a deep connection with them. Now I know why. You didn't grow up knowing anything about them.

I surmised, from the gossiping of Dodo and Naney, that the Vanderbilts were beyond rich, but who were they? It wasn't until I was about seven that I learned that my father had a sister named Gertrude Vanderbilt Whitney, but I had no idea where she lived. I didn't even find out that he had a daughter from a previous marriage, Cathleen, until I was fifteen.

That I have the name Vanderbilt has always felt like a huge mistake. I felt I was an imposter, a changeling, perhaps switched at birth, intruding under false pretenses. For me, this feeling has never gone away.

I had to look up the definition of *changeling*. In folklore it's a strange or ugly child left by faeries in the place of a pretty child. You said you were surrounded by love from Naney Morgan and Dodo. So what made you feel like that?

How to explain it?

I longed to connect with my mother, to feel that we belonged together, but I never seemed able to get her attention. I was always aware of her presence, though I had no intimacy with her that I can remember. I adored her beauty from a distance, but it was something I could never reach, never touch. She was a magical stranger.

I knew early on that Naney and Dodo were intensely preoccupied with my mother's comings and goings, nosey about what was happening in her part of the house. Because they watched her so closely and often whispered about her, it was clear to me it was my mother who was really in charge—*la maîtresse de la maison*, as the French would say. When you came right down to it, Naney and Dodo had no real power, so every moment felt perilous. We were all walking on eggshells.

I began to fear my mother. At times I'd cling to Dodo and Naney and cry for no apparent reason, unable to stop even when they tried to comfort me. How could Naney and Dodo really belong to me, and protect me, when they themselves were vassals of my mother? And if they weren't really in control, then who was I? Perhaps I didn't belong there at all, and it would be only a matter of time before I was discovered and snatched from my bed, thrown up to the ceiling, onto the

ANDERSON COOPER and
Gloria Vanderbilt

threatening shapes streaking across it from the headlights of
cars passing in the street below.

I can understand that you didn't know your mother, you saw
her only as an elusive, beautiful creature heading out with
her identical twin to cocktail parties and dinners, but why
did you fear her?

It's hard to understand—it has certainly
taken me a long time to make sense of it—but I think that
Naney and Dodo's anger and fear that I would be taken to
Germany began to seep into me. It was when I was lying in the
dark in bed at night, listening to them whispering, that the fear
began to take root. Something was amiss, something terrible
was about to happen, and it had to do with my mother—but
exactly what it was, I didn't know.

If I'd had a relationship with her, a connection to her, it
would have been different, but I had none. Naney and Dodo's
feelings toward her became my own, and my fear would only
grow in the coming years.

After a while, my mother became tired of all of Naney's
meddling and wanted to get some distance from her, so she sent
her to live in a separate apartment nearby. My grandmother
must have sensed that her power was under threat, which only
gave her more incentive to get me back to America.

We were moving around a lot throughout Europe, because my mother wanted to go to parties and meet people. After Paris, there was a rented house in Cannes—or, rather, two houses: the one where she stayed with Lady Nada Milford Haven and other friends and the one where I lived with Dodo.

Dodo and I then moved to a hotel in Montreux, Switzerland, before going on to Melton Mowbray, in England, for a Christmas visit with Aunt Thelma, who was married to Lord Furness. The marriage was not a happy one, and Thelma was in the midst of a long affair with Edward, Prince of Wales. He was a guest of honor at the Christmas gathering, and other visitors drifted in and out, making a big fuss over him because someday it was thought he would be king of England.

Of course, he later ended up abdicating the throne to marry Wallis Simpson. In fact, it was Thelma who introduced her friend Wallis to Prince Edward, asking her to "look after him" while she went on a trip in 1934. Wallis certainly did.

It was a festive holiday: every day a gala, with guests coming and going, one more exquisitely beautiful than the next. I'd glimpse my mother among them, there but nowhere near me.

One morning in our room, Dodo got up quickly and firmly locked the door leading into the hall. She then told me to sit down at the desk, handed me a pen, and placed a sheet of stationery in front of me. I could tell it was serious because her neck was flushed red as roast beef, which always happened when she was upset.

Her voice was suddenly that of a stranger, with a harsh tone I'd never heard before: "Your Naney wants to hear from you, and this is the letter you are going to write to her: 'Dear Naney, My mother said not to write but I am not paying any attention to her. She is a rare bease. Well, I will be in dear old New York soon. Love and kisses, Naney dear. Gloria.' "

What was going on? The door locked? Dodo so unlike herself? A letter to Naney who at that very moment was also a guest at Melton Mowbray, sitting in the room next to the one we were in, with a misspelling of *beast* that Dodo made me put in so it would look like I'd written the letter myself?

"No," I said, throwing the pen on the floor.

Dodo leaned down swiftly, picked it up, and shoved it back into my hand.

"Yes! Now! Right now! Naney will be very, very angry with us both if you do not do this now, *right now!*"

Dodo was shaking, too, but raising her voice, she pushed on, "She's in the next room *waiting* for me to take it to her, so no more questions. *Snap to it!*"

Confused, angry at Dodo, but most of all, angry at myself without knowing why, I did what I was told.

It was only later that I came to understand that this letter was a tiny piece in the puzzle·of partnership Naney and Dodo had formed to get me back to America with the Vanderbilts, where they believed I belonged. The letter surfaced later, in the custody case. It was obviously not something a child that age would have written, and it was used by my mother's lawyer, Nathan Burkan, in an attempt to prove Naney's manipulation of me, and her betrayal of her own daughter.

After our stay at Melton Mowbray, Dodo and I went to live in a rented house in the English countryside, before returning to the Savoy hotel in London. Then, suddenly, Naney, Dodo, and I were on a ship called the *Majestic*, sailing to America and the Vanderbilts.

I t's incredible to think that Naney Morgan, your grandmother, would plot against your mother, her own daughter, so that she would lose custody of you. What was her motivation?

I adored Naney when I was a child, but I really do believe she was mentally unbalanced. How else can one explain the events that followed? She had the intelligence and cunning of Machiavelli's Prince, and was capable of blowing up subways, if necessary, to achieve her plans. I've often wondered what kind of early experiences molded her into a feminine version of her idol, Napoléon. Would she reveal her secrets if we could confide in each other today? I think not.

Although an ardent Roman Catholic, Naney found her true God in money and social position. This may be part of the answer to the riddle of why she hatched the elaborate plot that made such a tangled mess of so many lives.

Naney was born Laura Delphine Kilpatrick in Santiago, Chile, in 1877. Her father was an infamous Civil War general, Hugh Judson Kilpatrick, who had been appointed consul general to Chile, and her mother, Luisa Valdivieso, was from a well-known Chilean family. I have some gold-tooled, red leather scrapbooks that Naney made specifically for pasting newspaper clippings of the hundreds of social events she attended over the years. Page after page details the occasions and names of those present, hers prominently featured.

Naney talked endlessly about Chilean socialites she had known, rambling on and on about this one and that one, always mentioning at some point that the Valdivieso family was related to Vincent of Loyola, the Catholic saint.

Naney was still unmarried at thirty-three when she came to America for the first time, with her mother. She would have been considered an "old maid," as back then most girls married in their teens. It was in New York City that she met a diplomat, Harry Hays Morgan. He was quite a catch, and they married soon after.

Naney maneuvered a meeting with President Taft, who was in office at the time, and charmed him into posting my grandfather as consul general in Lucerne, Switzerland. There she gave birth to a daughter, Consuelo; then a son, Harry Junior; and later to the twins, my mother and Thelma.

Naney adored all her family, but as her daughters grew, it was clear that the beautiful twins were the most likely to achieve the brilliant marriages she had envisioned for her girls, and for her own future protection as well.

When my mother married Reginald Vanderbilt in 1923, Naney was ecstatic. She was now linked to one of America's most prominent families. When I was born, nine months to the day later, she ensconced herself along with Dodo in my father's house on Seventy-Fourth Street and on Sandy Point Farm, in Newport, for the summer, which is where they were living when my father died.

So she schemed against her own daughter because of money and wanting you to be part of society in America?

Greed and ambition were a big part of it, but it wasn't until my mother became involved with Prince Friedel Hohenlohe that Naney sprang into action.

46

The prince had a title and came from a very distinguished family, but he didn't have money. Naney and Dodo considered him "a Count of no account," which wasn't true, but it's what Naney used to say about most of the men my mother spent time with. If he married my mother, what would they live on? My trust fund, of course, and I would be taken to live in the prince's castle in Germany. Perhaps Naney was also worried about the rise of Adolf Hitler, or her own financial position if she were no longer living with us.

So Naney decided it was time to get me back to America, where she believed I belonged, with the Vanderbilts—and who was more appropriate than my father's sister Gertrude Vanderbilt Whitney to take charge? Gertrude had a fortune, and her own children were all grown.

———

Gertrude Vanderbilt Whitney and her sister, Gladys, were the only surviving siblings of Reginald Vanderbilt. They had another brother, Alfred, who was a passenger on the ocean liner the RMS Lusitania when it was torpedoed by a German submarine in 1915. Alfred gave his life jacket to a woman on the ship who had a small child, even though he didn't know how to swim and knew there were no more lifeboats available. He drowned in the freezing cold water along with 1,197 other passengers

and crew members. His body was never found. He was
thirty-seven years old.

Gertrude was ahead of her time in many ways. One of
the richest women in America, she was an accomplished
sculptor, and in 1930 she founded the Whitney Museum
of American Art, which remains one of the most import-
ant contemporary art museums in the world.

My mother knew nothing about her aunt Gertrude
when she returned to America in 1932. She was an eight-
year-old girl coming to a country she had no memory of,
to meet a family that had not seen her since she was an
infant.

=====

When Dodo and I arrived in America, we
went straight to Newport, to stay at Oakland Farm, with my
cousin Bill Vanderbilt and his wife, who told me I could call
her Mummy Anne, as her own daughters did. I was thrilled.

It was the first time I had seen a mother and a father up
close. I'd always thought of Dodo as my mother and Naney
as my father, but here was a father who was actually a man.
They were all part of the "family" Dodo had told me I was
going to meet, but I didn't get to stay there long, certainly not
long enough to understand what family life could be like.
Naney wanted Aunt Gertrude to get to know me, so she

arranged for me to move to my aunt's estate in Old Westbury, New York.

I had met Gertrude only once, when I visited the Breakers, in Newport, with Mummy Anne. The Breakers was built for my father's parents, Cornelius and Alice Vanderbilt, by the architect Richard Morris Hunt in 1893. It was as large as a palace, with seventy rooms, but was referred to as "the cottage," and occupied only in the summer months. During the rest of the year, they lived in New York, in another mansion that took up the entire block of Fifth Avenue between Fifty-Seventh and Fifty-Eighth Streets. It was later torn down; the department store Bergdorf Goodman now stands in its place.

When I met Aunt Gertrude, I had no idea of the plans Naney and Dodo had been making for me and no hint of the important role my aunt would play in the rest of my life.

When I was a child, I remember looking at pictures of Gertrude, but I didn't understand who she was and how she was related to you.

Her appearance was striking. In the photographs, she was no longer young but she was dressed beautifully, her face often hidden under a large hat, and unlike other women of that time, she seemed always to be wearing pants.

I remember we spent several Thanksgivings when I was

a teenager at Gertrude's former estate in Old Westbury. The main house and its grounds had been sold off and turned into a private club, but her granddaughter lived in what had been Gertrude's studio. It was nice to meet those relatives, and they were always very gracious, but they were so different from the many members of my father's family I had met. Since we really saw them only once a year, I never got to know them very well.

What was Gertrude like?

Aunt Gertrude was gracious, charming, and steady, but distant, uncommunicative, and extremely reserved. Her demeanor and the clothes she wore were appropriate to every occasion, and she was always immaculate from head to toe.

She was so unlike fiery Naney Morgan, whose wardrobe was meager, and who usually appeared in a well-worn orange sweater and black suit. Naney was always going off on tangents and extravagantly smothering me with love.

The first time I met Aunt Gertrude she was wearing pants like a man! It was something of a shock. In those days women didn't wear what later came to be known as slacks. Gertrude favored men's pants fashioned by a tailor who appeared when summoned with fabrics from Italy for her selection: cashmeres, wools, silks, and taffetas in white, deliciously creamy.

She wore tailored shirts to complement each ensemble. I never saw her without masses of Vanderbilt pearls cascading down her neck or the pair of pearl and diamond bracelets, one on each wrist, which she left to Cathleen, my older half-sister, and me in her will.

Was the red hair a wig? Probably not, but that is how it seemed to me as a child. Her hair was always perfectly marcelled, curled in layers, not a wave out of place. It framed her face and was sprayed to stay put through any emergency. On summer days, she wore a jaunty hat of palest thin straw, in winter one of softest felt, with a ribbon of black grosgrain silk.

In the evening, before dinner, she would change into one or another of her floor-length gowns, fashioned of flowing silk or jersey, complementing the extreme slenderness of her body.

Despite her superb style and elegance, she couldn't come anywhere close to the movie star beauty of my mother. But she did have something my mother did not—the power money brings.

W hat was it like to suddenly meet all these relatives? Did it make you feel like any less of a changeling?

Actually, it made me feel more so. Mummy Anne and Cousin Bill had welcomed me in Newport as if I was one of them, but when I went to stay with Aunt Gertrude, her grown children, who lived in other houses on her estate, made me feel like an intruder and it was only a matter of time before I would be discovered and banished.

Naney spent the summer in New York, installed in a one-room apartment at the Hotel Fourteen in Manhattan, and I hadn't heard anything from my mother for months. Then suddenly I learned she had also arrived in New York and Dodo and I were sent to live with her in a house on Seventy-Second Street, between Fifth and Madison Avenues.

You hadn't heard from your mother for months? Transatlantic telephone calls were new, but she hadn't written to you? What was it like to see her again?

It was strange seeing her after so long. When Dodo and I first entered the house, she was sitting in the living room with her older sister, Consuelo. My mother looked as ravishing as ever: long nails lacquered mahogany red; raven hair coiled tenderly in a chignon at the nape of her neck; her passive beauty as exquisite as it was the last time we met. But there wasn't much of a reunion. She was polite as always, and we hugged each other, but neither of us could think of what to say. Dodo and I were shown up to the top floor of the house, which was to be our domain.

I've since learned that Naney had been in communication with Aunt Gertrude, telling her about my mother's lifestyle in Europe and how she was spending money from my trust on herself instead of on me. Gertrude had then told Surrogate Foley, who was in charge of my finances, that I was staying in Newport with relatives that summer, so he cut my mother's allowance dramatically. My mother must have realized that unless she were living with me, she would have no money. So that is why she came back to New York.

———

Realizing she was vulnerable without parental rights over my mother, my grandmother decided to petition the Surrogate Court to name her sole guardian of my mother, which she hadn't thought to do previously. Naney Morgan decided it was time to act and filed a complaint with the court against her daughter, claiming that she was an unfit mother.

———

I didn't know anything about what my mother or Naney were doing, but one day during the first week at my mother's house, I overheard my aunt Consuelo saying, "First thing you must do is get rid of the nurse. What that child needs is a German fräulein."

Consuelo was telling my mother to fire Dodo! It was a gunshot into my gut. If Dodo were taken from me, I would die. With those words, the fear of my mother, which had for years been only a vague feeling, exploded into panic and terror, burrowing deep into my heart.

If she had the power to take Dodo, my true mother, away from me, then she was capable of anything.

I ran up the stairs to find Dodo, but I was really running to a cliff's edge, and when I came to it, I didn't stop. I took a giant leap, falling, falling forever into the fear. I loved my mother, but I hated her.

I hugged Dodo, exploding between sobs, trying to get out what I had just heard. *Get rid of the nurse!*

"Gloria, listen," Dodo said. "We are going to go down the stairs. If asked, say that we are going to the park. It will be all right, but you must stop crying. You must act as if nothing has happened. If you can do that, we can slip out of the house. Everything will be all right."

Dodo knew Aunt Gertrude had the power to put right whatever was wrong. Casually down the stairs we went, past my mother and Consuelo, still deep in conversation, so engrossed they didn't notice us slip by. Once outside, we headed straight for Aunt Gertrude's studio in Greenwich Village.

When we got there, I lay down on the sofa, a sobbing, hysterical child, choking on pain and fear and clinging to my aunt as she tried to calm me.

"You don't have to go back to your mother's," my aunt said. "You can stay with me."

And there it was. This was the moment Naney and Dodo had dreamed of and planned for. The moment that changed my life.

I was safe, or so I thought—but the fear of my mother would never go away.

Two

When she discovered where my mother was, my grandmother accused Gertrude Vanderbilt Whitney of imprisoning her child. She served Gertrude with court papers ordering her to return my mother, but Gertrude refused and, with Naney Morgan and Dodo on her side, decided to fight for custody.

Lawyers were hired, a trial date was set, and both sides began preparing for a court fight unlike any the country had ever seen.

Before it began, Surrogate Foley, my mother's legal guardian, tried to convince my grandmother not to go to trial.

"Do you know what a trial of this caliber can do?" he asked her. "There will be so much dirt in the press that it will drag you and the child through a mire of infamy that will cling to her as long as she lives."

Naney Morgan tried a different appeal to her daughter: "If you permit her to live with Mrs. Whitney, I feel sure Mrs. Whitney will give you fifty thousand dollars a year for life."

But my grandmother decided to go to trial anyway, to fight for custody of a child she barely knew.

The trial began on October 1, 1934, when my mother was ten years old. It was presided over by Judge John Francis Carew, and was a global media sensation. More than one hundred reporters packed the courtroom for what many papers called "The Trial of the Century."

After showing up at Aunt Gertrude's studio sobbing, I didn't go back to my mother's house, and instead went to live on Gertrude's estate in Old Westbury, on Long Island. I was enrolled at the nearby Greenvale School, and every day Freddy, her chauffeur, would drive me there in a gray Rolls-Royce. I hadn't gone to school in Paris, so I was placed in a grade below my age group.

My aunt told me to call her Auntie Ger, and so I did. I thought she was very old, but she was only fifty-nine, which seems very young as I sit here right now.

I now understand why she had felt compelled to act with regard to my custody. She was doing what she believed to be the right thing. She must have thought, "Something is terribly wrong about the way my niece is being treated by her mother to make her sob so hysterically."

I didn't understand then how difficult it must have been for her, how courageous and brave to take me, a related, but unknown child, into her life. She was the most private of women, yet she must have realized that she would be sucked into a very public custody battle.

Auntie Ger lived in Manhattan during the week and came to Old Westbury only on weekends. Dodo would rev me up to be ready for her arrival. When we heard the car coming up the driveway, I was to rush down the ten steps, holding on to the bannister, throw my arms around her, and cry out, "Auntie Ger, Auntie Ger! I'm so happy to see you!" And it was true. I was.

We would have lunches and dinner together in the dining room overlooking the lawn and meadows beyond. The meals were served by William, the butler, with the second footman standing discreetly nearby. It was the kind of lifestyle you see now only on *Downton Abbey*, but it was a strain knowing what to talk about with my aunt. I longed to find out more about my father, but I didn't quite know how to bring him up. She had a sculptured bust of him, by Jo Davidson, in an alcove in her bedroom, but she never mentioned my father's name to me. Not once.

Sensing I was often at a loss as to how to behave in the social situations that were part of this new world I suddenly found myself in at Auntie Ger's, Dodo gave me *Emily Post's Book of Etiquette*. The charmed life I read about fascinated me.

I went to bed much earlier than my aunt did, and I'd lie awake (with the door half open because I was still afraid of the dark) and listen to her voice as she came up the stairs calling out to her dachshund, "Come along, Comet. Come along, Comet." I'd hold my breath, wondering if she would stop by my door and call out to me, *"Buona notte"* as she had the night before. And she always did.

I am surprised your mother decided to go to trial. She could have taken the money Gertrude was offering and gone back to Europe. It's not like she spent any time with you; she barely knew you. Why do you think she fought for custody?

I've often wondered that. Of course, I didn't know at the time that Auntie Ger had used Naney as an intermediary to offer my mother fifty thousand dollars a year for life if she would let me stay in Old Westbury. That was a huge amount of money in those days.

I suspect she didn't accept because not only would the Vanderbilt family have thought poorly of her, but there would have been nasty gossip about her. My mother, well trained by Naney, had achieved the pinnacle of social success by becoming Mrs. Reginald Claypoole Vanderbilt.

If she had taken the money, Newport and New York society would likely not have reacted sympathetically, and she would have been ostracized, a story line Edith Wharton often explored in her novels.

I also suspect that she believed she would win the custody case. William Randolph Hearst had become a friend and was fully behind her, giving her favorable press coverage, and the American public was on her side, at least in the beginning. People found it inconceivable that a child would testify in court that she didn't want to live with her own mother.

I have no doubt she was completely unaware of her failings, her lack of interest in me, and her inability from the beginning to bond with her blob of an infant daughter. As she grew older, she was proud to have photographs taken of us together, but simply because she believed it reflected well on her.

I think she considered herself a good mother—that is, if she thought about it much at all.

It's hard to believe she could have thought of herself as a good mother, but I guess narcissistic people don't have much sense of what they are really like or how they make other people feel.

It's sad to think of you at that age, surrounded by people with so many competing interests. Even though Naney Morgan and Dodo clearly loved you, it was very manipulative of them to try to get you away from your mother and back to America.

You must have felt so scared with all that was happening. Fear is one of the things I hated about being a child, particularly after Daddy died. I always felt a lack of control over what might happen next. Just as you said you did as a child, I felt like we were adrift on a raft without a rudder.

We had moved out of the house on Sixty-Seventh Street when I was six and were living in an apartment near the UN when he died. Soon after, we moved to another apartment, in a building nearby. At the time, it didn't seem unusual that we pulled up stakes and relocated so often, or that you were constantly redecorating rooms wherever we lived. It must have felt very normal to you to move so much, since you spent your childhood frequently traveling around Europe. No place could ever have given you the feeling of stability you were seeking.

The fear I felt so often as a child is something I've worked a long time to rid myself of, and it's why I so enjoy the confidence that age and experience bring.

Did you know your mother was going to fight in court to get you back and that you would be asked to decide between her and your aunt?

Auntie Ger never mentioned the trial or my testifying. Not once. One day, we were joined at lunch by Frank Crocker, Auntie Ger's lawyer, and he soon became a frequent guest. I had met him before and, in a moment of confusion and sadness, had asked him if he could be my father. He looked at me, stunned, dismay in his eyes, then stuttered and stumbled out of the room. Ever since then, I called him Fatso, but only secretly to myself.

Why was he now appearing at our lunches? I wondered. It was after the third visit that I discovered the answer. Auntie Ger left me alone with him in the living room, and he went straight to the point, informing me that my mother wished me to live with her and not my aunt. Did I want to go back to my mother or remain living with Auntie Ger?

"Here, here at Auntie Ger's, Auntie Ger's," I said, then started crying. "Here with Dodo, Dodo, Dodo!"

He went to the French doors and stood looking out over the lawn, with his back to me. I sobbed and sobbed, and the big fat blob turned and came toward me. I got up to run from the room, but he moved fast for my hand and pulled me onto the sofa beside him.

"Well, well, that's settled then. There's nothing to be afraid of. Listen to me and stop that crying. Listen to me. All that has to be done is for you to make your wishes known to the nice judge, and he will arrange it so that you will live with your Aunt Gertrude for as long as you like."

"Forever and ever?" I cried out.

"Of course. Forever and ever."

The next time Crocker came to Old Westbury was not for lunch but for the first of many sessions going over what was about to happen. He told me that if I was to remain with Auntie Ger, the law required that I appear in court to meet Judge Carew and tell him in my own words why I didn't want to live with my mother.

It was an interesting question. I knew if I were sent back to my mother, I would never see Dodo, my true mother, ever again. Dodo was there with me in Old Westbury, sleeping in the room across from mine, and Auntie Ger was friendly toward her, so I had no doubt that it couldn't be like that forever. Crocker was hardly a person to confide in, though, so I didn't tell him that Dodo was the real reason I wanted to stay with my aunt. Of course he didn't have a clue that I had begun to fear my mother because of the atmosphere Naney and Dodo created around her, a fear that took hold in me early on.

Crocker told me to tell Judge Carew a story that Naney made up about Prince Friedel Hohenlohe extinguishing his cigarette on my arm. It wasn't true of course. I had met the prince only once, in the living room of our house in Paris. He was very formal and polite, and he was smoking, but he certainly never tried to harm me. I assumed Crocker had heard the story from Naney, but luckily it never came up in my conversation with the judge. It took a lot of effort to remember all the things Crocker told me to say:

"I am happy living with Auntie Ger because, with my

mother, we always kept moving around so much and now I have a real home."

"It's been great fun to start going to school and have friends my own age to play with."

And so on.

Auntie Ger was not at the house the day I had to go to court to have the "little chat," as I was told, with the judge.

I was dreading it and went over the lines I'd rehearsed with Crocker again and again. I hoped to God I wouldn't forget anything.

When the time came, Freddy, my aunt's chauffeur, drove me to Manhattan with a private detective in the front seat. There were crowds of people waiting in the street outside the courthouse, and photographers taking pictures as I got out and proceeded up the steps flanked by more detectives. I could hear people shouting my name, some of them telling me to stick up for my mother.

Paralyzed with terror, I went into Judge Carew's private chambers. It was just the two of us and, at a distance, a stenographer with pretty pink nail polish who clicked our conversation onto a little machine. The judge spoke softly and was friendly, and I was careful to answer his questions as I had been instructed. The meeting was short and it wasn't so terrible after all. I left knowing I had done well and proud of myself for not flubbing my lines. The future was assured.

Driving back to Old Westbury, I knew Auntie Ger would not be waiting for me, but Dodo would, and that was all that mattered. She and I would live together happily ever after. Or so I thought.

T he other day I watched an old black-and-white newsreel of you arriving at the courthouse. I found it online. A mob of private detectives in overcoats and fedoras surrounds you. Your head is down and you are walking quickly into the building. None of these men is looking at you or seems connected to you in any way. One jumps in front of the cameras with his arms stretched wide in a ridiculous attempt to block you from being photographed. I kept watching it over and over. You were only ten years old, and though you were surrounded by guards, you were all alone.

I saw another newsreel of you leaving the court. An announcer intones, almost gleefully, "Frightened by the curious crowds, Little Gloria jumps into her aunt's limousine. . . . Mooooney isn't everything!"

Did anyone talk to you about what was happening at the trial each day? Did you know what was going on?

Auntie Ger's estate was a fortress, shielded from the world and the publicity of the trial, but I knew from seeing the crowds outside the courthouse and hearing people shout at me that the public was hungry for daily tabloid updates. It was a drama that had everything: sex, scandal, glamour, and big, big money at stake. In the coverage, we became like mythical characters in a soap opera—except, of course, we were real.

I had no idea what was happening each day in court. Neither Auntie Ger nor anyone else talked to me about it, but one day I overheard Bridie, the cook, gossiping with William, the butler, as they pored over a front-page story about the trial in the *Daily News*, and I learned that Judge Carew had closed the proceedings to the press and public because of something unspeakable that had been revealed about my mother.

Marie, the maid who had worked for her in Paris, was brought to New York by Auntie Ger's lawyers to testify that she had seen my mother and Lady Nada Milford Haven in bed together making love.

I didn't know what homosexuality was. The words *gay* and *lesbian* weren't in use at the time, and even if they had been, I would never have encountered them. Whatever it was, I could tell it was something heinous that must be my fault, something that I, too, may have inherited. Could this be the hole in my heart that I'd always felt?

I was in high school when I first heard that your mother was accused of being a lesbian. I wanted to ask you about it,

but I sensed it disturbed you, and I didn't want to upset you by bringing it up.

It was part of what scared me about telling you I was gay when I was twenty-one. I had all the normal feelings of trepidation about coming out to you, but it was largely because of the allegations against her; I wasn't sure how you would react.

I remember I once told you that I thought sexual orientation was partly genetic, and you quickly and firmly disagreed. Your reaction surprised me because the idea clearly upset you, yet so many of your closest friends were gay, and were such a big part of our lives growing up.

Was your mom a lesbian?

Yes, she was, but she also had affairs with men. I think that for some people sexuality is fluid. Much later she told me her one great love was Prince Friedel Hohenlohe, but she had been unable to wed him because Surrogate Foley, who controlled my trust fund, said that no part of it could be used to finance a second marriage and neither of them had enough money to support themselves in the style to which they were accustomed. By marrying the prince, she would have become a "Serene Highness," which no doubt would have been important to her, as well as marrying the love of her life.

After her engagement to the prince ended, her longest and most passionate relationship was with Lady Nada Milford

Haven, who was related to the Russian royal family and married to Prince George of Battenberg, a great-grandson of Queen Victoria. Fascinating, glamorous, mesmerizing in her zaftig splendor, Nada had a mop of tousled red and orange hair and lacquered her nails the same shade of mahogany as my mother. She wore dresses of soft, flowing fabrics and carried a cigarette in an ivory holder. Her face was startlingly alive, and she had a great verve for life.

My passive and shy mother was attracted by the contrast in their personalities. She became another person when she was with Nada: she appeared happy. I didn't know it then, but I realize now it was because they were madly in love.

When I was seven, during a stay in London, I once spied on my mother and Nada. Through a half-open door, I saw them sitting together on a sofa, arms around each other, laughing, and whispering in front of a glowing fire.

My mother, turning suddenly, caught me staring. "Close the door," she called out, annoyed. "There's a draft coming in. Run on out and play."

Something was going on, but it both confused and frightened me.

My mother was proud of her relationship with Nada, who was constantly by her side. They even traveled together, guests of William Randolph Hearst and Marion Davies at San Simeon, Hearst's fabled ranch.

ANDERSON COOPER and
Gloria Vanderbilt

When the story about my mother's relationship with Nada became public, it was a terrible scandal. In 1934, being gay was considered evil. It was a crime. Gay people could be, and were, arrested, imprisoned, and institutionalized.

I heard that the doors of the courtroom had been closed and blocked to the public because of a revelation concerning my mother, but I didn't know what it was, just that it was very terrible—as terrible as murder. Later, I pieced together that it wasn't murder, but in the minds of many back then, it was considered even more unspeakable.

The allegation that my beautiful mother was a lesbian, clamped down on my ten-year-old heart, squeezing it hard, as if with a nutcracker. Pain scrambled my brain, sucking me into a whirlpool of vile thoughts. I didn't understand what it meant, but I knew it wasn't like the love between Jeanette Macdonald and Nelson Eddy in *Maytime* or any of the other movies I would come to obsess over. It was something chill and bitter, confirming all the fears I already had about my mother.

There was no one I could speak to about this. I shut myself in and tried desperately to put the pieces of my heart and mind back into some kind or order. It was a long haul because I obsessively worried that I, too, would grow up to be like my mother: a lesbian.

When boys came into the picture it was an incredible relief. I was a girl who loved boys, not a "freak" who loved girls.

74

I tell you all this so you understand why it took me so long, until my thirties, to understand that there is nothing strange or peculiar about being gay or lesbian. Love between two women, or two men, is precisely the same as love between a woman and a man.

W hen I told you I was gay, it must have brought up a lot of your feelings about your own mother. It makes sense to me now. I remember the day I finally decided to speak to you about it. I was really nervous, but felt like I couldn't wait any longer.

I had come out to my friends while I was in high school, but had waited to tell you. When I graduated from college, I decided it was silly to avoid it any longer. I assumed you'd figured it out, because you had never asked me about girls, and I'd had a boyfriend all through college whom you knew very well. He slept over at our apartment often, and I thought you must have guessed he wasn't just a friend. Still, when I went into your room that day, I was very nervous.

"There is something I need to talk to you about," I said, sitting down next to you on your bed. "I think I'm gay."

I immediately regretted the wording. I didn't *think* I was gay. I *knew* I was. I had known it since I was six or seven years old.

"You do?" you asked, but it wasn't really a question. You were biding your time, absorbing what I had just said.

I explained that I had felt this way all my life, and that I was happy about being gay.

You said my boyfriend was always welcome, and then, after a slight pause, you said, "Don't make any definite decisions."

It wasn't really what I expected you to say, and I wondered if perhaps I should have been more direct, but then I decided to just let it sink in for a while with you.

Did you know I was gay before I told you?

I may have occasionally suspected you were gay, but it only floated in and out of my mind along with my unresolved feelings about my mother's sexuality and my remembered terror as a child that I might have inherited the same orientation as well as the alcoholism of my father.

If you were gay, I thought, it would be my fault and an indication that I had been a bad parent.

When you said, "I think I'm gay," you left it open, as if you were not yet certain. We all go through adolescence with conflicting emotions, and I wasn't sure if you meant you were or might be. Then you left the room soon after without continuing the conversation.

When you left I was shattered, because I remembered something I had said offhandedly years before when we were talking about one of your friends who might be gay: "I would feel I had failed as a parent if one of my children were gay." It was an ignorant remark, and I had no idea it would or could have anything to do with you. I wish you had known those words came from feelings I still harbored about the revelation about my mother in the trial.

It took great courage for you to confide in me, and I wished you had stayed longer so that we could have talked more, but I understood that after telling me something so important you needed time alone to get back to yourself.

A ctually, I thought that after the big reveal you might be the one who needed some time alone. But I knew once you got over the initial surprise you would be supportive. As I said, so many of your friends were gay, and they were always coming over for dinners and parties.

I didn't remember your saying that you'd feel like a failure if one of your children were gay, but I do remember something else you once said that made a strong and positive impression on me.

We were waiting for guests to arrive one night for a dinner at our house when I was around eleven. I asked you about the theater director José Quintero and his partner, Nick, who were coming that evening.

"They are just like a married couple," you explained to me. Of course, this was 1979, and in the eyes of the law and most Americans, they certainly were not anything like a married couple, but I never forgot that you believed they were. That is why I knew you would be okay with it when I finally told you I was gay.

Well, I hope you know that I am more than "okay" with it; I *rejoice* that you are gay! It is part of what makes you the person you are, and I am so glad that you have found someone who makes you happy. I wouldn't want you any other way, even if that were possible, which it most certainly is not.

Today it is still hard to believe how far we have come, with same-sex marriage legal in all of our United States. Of course, it is only the beginning. True equality still has a long way to go both here at home and around the world.

After the light dawned on me in my thirties, I often secretly wished I, too, had been born gay. My closest friends have always been women, and I certainly understand them more than I do men, but it was not to be. Some people have all the luck!

———

In the wake of the headline-making revelations about my grandmother's relationship with Lady Nada Mil-

ford Haven, public opinion began to shift in favor of my mother's aunt.

After seven weeks of testimony, the Matter of Vanderbilt, *as the case was officially called, came to a close.*

Judge Carew awarded custody of my mother to Gertrude Vanderbilt Whitney. My grandmother Gloria Morgan Vanderbilt would be allowed to have supervised visits with my mom on weekends and some holidays.

The judge also made a ruling that my ten-year-old mother could never have predicted, one she thought she might not survive.

———

Nothing worked out in the custody trial as I imagined. Though my mother lost, her lawyers said that Dodo had influenced me against her, and Judge Carew decreed that Dodo could no longer have any contact with me. She was fired, and I was not allowed to see her or even speak to her on the phone. I didn't know where she had gone. I was ten years old, and I thought I would die. It was the worst thing that could ever happen to me—or so I thought until Carter died.

Up until the judge's ruling, I had been secure in the knowledge that I was loved, not by my mother, but by Dodo and Naney, who were my real parents. While they were by my side

I knew for sure that I was the center of their world. Never had a child been so cherished, loved, and adored.

When I was separated from Dodo by the judge, part of me did die. Without Dodo at Auntie Ger's, I felt like a lowly, miserable creature who had committed a crime, only I didn't know what it was.

Unexpectedly tiptoeing into this strange new world appeared the changeling, keeping its head up by treading water, wee paws slipping through the marshy meadow, a mouse not shaking the grass, desperately trying and failing to remain unnoticed, all the while dying and straining to please those around me, but most of all the queen herself, Auntie Ger.

I started stuttering, and dreaded each school day, especially Lit class, when I would inevitably have to stand and stumble through a poem in front of everyone. I recently came across a Greenvale School report card. Below all the C's and B's was a handwritten note from my teacher, "She will succeed— eventually." (See? Everything can turn out all right if you just hang in there!)

I put on weight and hated myself. I was a hippo on an island, alone, floundering around, clutching at reeds so as not to slip into the hostile sea.

What mattered beauty? What mattered perfection? They were the attributes gifted only to my mother and Aunt Thelma, which I would never achieve.

Doubt about who I was spread into my veins. If I didn't know, then how could Auntie Ger or anyone else? I longed to please and be accepted by her and her grown children, these strange new relatives I had not even known existed, and this desire for acceptance took hold of me with a grip that wouldn't let go.

This is a terrible flaw that you, Anderson, thank God, do not have. From birth, you have been cherished and adored. Even as an adult, the need to please others coursed through my veins. Pleasing a person flooded me with warmth, which made me feel successful, and momentarily safe. But it never lasted.

Trying to please everyone all the time never works. It leads to hating oneself and then hating oneself even more when one later tries to assert one's authority.

Today, I am still tempted to be drawn into old patterns. Someone will ask me to do something, work on a painting for them or give an interview, and I have to force myself to pause and question: Do I really want to do this? But whether the answer is yes or no, at least I know the answer will be one that is true to my desires.

It is stunning to think that the judge would take away the person you cared most about, the woman who'd raised you from the moment you were born. She was your mother certainly more than your biological mother ever was.

To have gone through all that you did, just to keep Dodo by your side, only to have her removed so suddenly and thoughtlessly—it's awful.

I remember when my nanny, May McLinden, who had been with me from the time I was born, left. I was inconsolable and I was *fifteen*, old enough not to need her as I once had. With Dodo exiled from your life, you must have felt so alone, more than ever before. Was there anyone you could turn to for support?

Dodo was banished, but I could still see Naney, and every night, promptly at 6:30 p.m., I was allowed to call her room at the Hotel Fourteen in Manhattan. Volunteer 5-6000. I'll never forget that phone number.

The judge had the power to send Dodo away, but he couldn't stop me from talking to my grandmother, even though she had played the key role in the effort to turn me against my mother.

That call was the lifeline that got me through the day. I knew she would always be there. Her voice leaped through the receiver as I held the phone close to my ear, "Hello, darling mine!" That is how she always greeted me.

We'd chat about this and that, and I hated having to hang up when it was time to say good night. Occasionally she came out to stay at Old Westbury when Auntie Ger was there. Naney loved to gossip about parties she had attended with my Grandfather Morgan when he was an ambassador in Europe. She'd go on endlessly in Spanish-accented English, a steady stream of banter about royalty, dropping names that meant nothing to me and certainly bored Auntie Ger.

I adored her and her visits, until one day, when I was fifteen and had met a boy named Geoffrey Jones. In love with him, I wanted to share my happiness with Naney, and told her that we planned to get married someday. But instead of being happy, she trembled with fury.

"Listen to me, little one: you are a *Vanderbilt* and can *never* marry anyone with the name *Jones*."

I became hysterical. The intensity of my reaction startled and frightened her.

She tried to calm me. "There, there, little one," she whispered, quickly putting her arms around me. "What's the matter? What's upsetting you? There, there, don't cry."

But it was too late. I never stopped loving her, but from that day on, it wasn't the same between us. When I became an adult, I saw her less and less often, fearful that any disagreement between us would topple me off the tightrope on which I so gingerly kept a grip. To move forward, to not fall off and be destroyed, took all the energy I had.

When Stan and Chris were born, Naney was ecstatic, and though I didn't accompany them on their weekly visits to see her at the Hotel Fourteen, I encouraged their affection for her.

She died in 1956. Her rambling final words were, "Did you get the ice cream for the babies?"

It wasn't until after her death that I learned she had reconciled with my mother at some point after the custody trial. My mother and Thelma were at Naney's bedside when she died, and she left both of them substantial sums in her will, but she never mentioned my mother to me after the trial, not once.

Geoff Jones was my first great love, but my first crush was for a boy named Johnny Delehanty. He was several years older than me, outgoing, at ease with himself, and divinely handsome as well. I was very shy then, if you can believe it. I literally would get weak in the knees every time I saw him.

Once, when my school friends Betty Lewis and Cynthia Ellis stayed overnight at Auntie Ger's, we sneaked out to meet Johnny and his chums, who picked us up past the estate's driveway and took us to Rothmann's restaurant. Auntie Ger had a watchman named Sharkey who caught us on our way out, but he never said anything to her or anyone else. We never thought about the danger, or the horrendous position my aunt would have been in with my guardian, Surrogate Foley, had this been discovered.

At Rothmann's we sat in a banquette drinking ginger ale for half an hour or so—then Johnny drove us back and we sneaked back into the house and into our beds. I had endless fantasies of Johnny and me getting married and living in a cottage like the ones I could see from the car window when I was driven into New York in my aunt's car. I would write Johnny's name next to mine over and over again,

"Delehanty. Gloria Delehanty. Mrs. John Bradley Delehanty. Mrs. John B. Delehanty."

His name was inexpressibly magical.

He was killed in an automobile accident during his freshman year at Cornell. His was the first death of someone I had been close to, and the first funeral I ever attended. It was inconceivable that Johnny could die. Death didn't exist, except as a word in a dictionary. It's what happened to old people. It had nothing to do with him.

I kept Johnny's letters, which I still have, and a framed photograph of him hangs today in my studio. He looks so young, but at fifteen, he was so much older in my eyes. I grieved, but after a time he faded into the landscape—and with him, the reality of death.

I've never heard you use the tightrope image before, but I understand what you mean. I think we are so alike in our desire to always move forward. It's something I think about all the time. I don't know that it's the healthiest way to live, but it is absolutely at the core of what I believe I need to do. I remember learning years ago that sharks have to keep moving forward to stay alive; it's the only way they can force water through their gills and breathe. Ever since, that is how I've imagined myself: a shark gliding through dark, silent seas.

For more than two decades now, I've moved constantly from one place to another, one story to the next, never allowing myself to slow down for long. I've worried that if I become too self-reflective or too mired in the pain of the past, the losses of Carter and Daddy, I will no longer be able to function, no longer be able to breathe.

It says something about the difference between us that you imagine yourself on a tightrope, constantly at risk of falling, and I see myself as a shark. I do not have a shark's thick skin, or the hunter's instinct, but there are times I wish I did. What is interesting to me is that you have always been able to keep going forward and at the same time have remained vulnerable. I worry that I have shut myself off to feeling, numbed myself so that I am not weighted down. I don't want to be numb, but it's hard to move forward constantly and to feel at the same time.

I don't think you really see yourself as a shark. It is not in your nature. If it were, you would be a businessman or a lawyer or in some other profession where ruthlessness and cunning are required. You are a storyteller, and though you may wish at times that you didn't feel pain, the fact that you continually put yourself in situations where you will, and where you can help others feel as well, speaks volumes about who and what you really are.

I could have hardened myself after Dodo was banished, but something in me made me decide not to. I chose to keep moving forward, but also to remain true to myself. I did become even more wary of my mother however. It was because of her that Dodo was taken from me.

When Judge Carew made his ruling in the custody trial, he also decreed I had to visit my mother on weekends. When I would see her, I was accompanied by private detectives, and a new governess named Eleanor Walsh. Out of all the governesses who came into and left my life after Dodo was dismissed, she was the best. She let me call her Tootsie Eleanor.

Every weekend my mother took us both to lunch at the Sherry-Netherland hotel. She always asked for a demitasse coffee after dessert and a glass of brandy, and then ordered one after another for what seemed an eternity, before she would ask for the check and we could leave.

Sundays, we went to Mass together at St. Francis Church, accompanied by a police car using its siren to get us through the crowds that gathered to ogle us. Though the trial was over, the public's fascination with my mother and me was not. To be less conspicuous, we were ushered up to the balcony inside the church, where the organ was. I'd sit with my mother on one side and Tootsie Eleanor on the other. My mother always became faint at some point during the Mass and would put her head between her knees so as not to keel over and pass out, but Tootsie was a registered nurse, so I knew that if anything happened, she'd be able to take care of her.

Who was the biggest influence on you as a teenager? I've always had the feeling that after the custody case you basically raised yourself.

What influences most people growing up is the reflection they have of themselves from a parent or parents. That was not the case for me when I was a teenager. The only reflection I saw of myself was a blob of nothing staring back at me in the mirror.

Even though I feared and often hated my mother, secretly I held a tiny hope that someday I might get her attention by growing up to be as beautiful as she was. She'd love me then— wouldn't she?

There were no role models in my life whom I could confide in. Dodo and Naney had surrounded me with their full attention and love, but they were not what today we call "mentors." Nor were Auntie Ger or Surrogate James Foley, who was my legal guardian until I was twenty-one.

The only real role models I had were characters in movies or books or on the radio. How shallow to have to admit that many of my childhood values were formed in large part by Busby Berkeley musicals, by Dick Powell singing to Joan Blondell, "By a waterfall, I'm calling *you*-oo-uu-oo-ooo."

Years later, when Frank Sinatra and I were dating, we dined once with Joan Blondell. I longed to tell her how influential she had been in my childhood, but when I tried, it was too complicated to explain why.

I had seen my first movie in 1935, when I was eleven. It was *Becky Sharp*, with Miriam Hopkins, and it premiered at Radio City Music Hall, where I climbed the winding steps up to the reserved seats in the mezzanine.

Before the movie, the famous tenor Jan Peerce appeared onstage and sang "The Bluebird of Happiness." When he sang, "Be like I . . . Hold your head up high . . . Till you find a bluebird of happiness," I almost fainted with the thrill. My soul soared into the thunderous applause. Yes! Yes! Happiness. There is somewhere a bluebird of happiness, and I will find it. I can, and I will. If I don't, I will die.

The glamour of it all was mesmerizing. It was the grown-up world of beauty and fantasy I longed to belong to. I melted back into my seat, torn between looking around at the ornate theater and watching what was happening in the film, although, at my age, I really didn't have a clue about the shenanigans on-screen.

I went back to Auntie Ger's house breathless, eager to see more movies, but I had to wait a long time. She only occasionally permitted me to watch films, and only ones she considered appropriate for my age.

My mother was more lenient. When I started weekend visits with her, she let Tootsie Eleanor take me go to the movies anytime I wanted. It was heaven for me, and for my mother, too, I imagine. It gave her a break from pretending everything was hunky-dory between us.

There were dozens of movies to choose from. All it took was a quick jaunt through Central Park to the West Side, where the theaters stood all in a row. If we managed to scoot out early from the endless lunch at the Sherry-Netherland, we could squeeze in a double feature, hopping from one theater and right into another.

With luck we'd hit a movie with Kay Francis, a famous actress I secretly thought resembled my mother. It was a thrilling communication, sitting silently in the almost empty theater, imagining that the woman on the screen was my mother and that we were together, having a much better time than we did when we actually were. Sounds weird, but that's how it was.

I recently rediscovered the Andy Hardy movies of the 1930s, starring a teenage Mickey Rooney. I had forgotten how these movies captivated me in my adolescence. Andy Hardy had a mom and a dad, Judge Jim Hardy. They lived in a house surrounded by a picket fence.

Mesmerized by the daily lives of this family, I discovered that this was what it could be like and what I wanted.

I loved best the scenes when Andy, seeking advice and reassurance, would knock on his dad's door. His father was always available, never too preoccupied with serious matters to have heart-to-heart talks with his son. He gave him sage advice, solving his problems with the wisdom of ultimate authority. I didn't realize it then, but these films held a secret message for me: if Dad is there, everything is safe.

I no longer puzzle over why, throughout my life, I have left men who loved me and whom I loved in return. Nothing ever felt safe, and though it was unfair of me, it felt wiser to abandon them before they abandoned me.

As I told you before, I was born with a hole in my heart. Sometimes a shock of wind whistles through it. It can never be completely filled.

Why am I telling you this? Because I'm hoping it may in some measure help you understand the roots from which my failings come, and the perseverance and strength it has taken to get me through ninety-one years to where I am now, standing unafraid, free and clear.

All those movies I saw provided my education. I believed that what appeared on the screen was how it was going to be when I grew up, and I couldn't wait for the reality of it to begin. When it finally did, it was quite a shock to discover it wasn't like that. No, not at all.

Back at Auntie Ger's, I started listening to "Uncle Don's" radio program, about Little Orphan Annie, who had been adopted by a billionaire she called Daddy Warbucks. Immediately I identified with Annie. If she survived, so could I. Auntie Ger was my Daddy Warbucks.

At fourteen, though, out went Orphan Annie and in galloped Jo March from Louisa May Alcott's *Little Women*. I loved the book, and when Katharine Hepburn portrayed Jo in the movie, I was over the moon. That was who I wanted to be, and I wasn't alone. All my schoolmates and cousins craved to be Jo, and we wouldn't settle for any of Jo's siblings—not even Amy, the pretty one—so we finally agreed to stop squabbling and we all started calling ourselves Jo.

Later, when Sidney Lumet and I were married, he directed Katharine Hepburn in *Long Day's Journey into Night*. I never told him why I didn't visit the set. I didn't want to meet her, not even after the movie had wrapped and she came to visit our apartment.

W hy didn't you want to meet her? She had been so important to you, and probably would have loved to hear the story.

Because, in a secret place inside me, the unworthy, fat girl of thirteen still had the grip of a tiger.

When Hepburn arrived, I was in my studio, which was next to the elevator. I could hear her voice as Sidney greeted her at the front door, but I didn't come out, and she left without our meeting. I felt unworthy at thirty-eight to shake Katharine Hepburn's hand. Unworthy at ninety-one? Indeed, no. Now I would feel worthy to give her a big hug, but it's taken me a long time to get here, and I congratulate myself on finally making it.

Y our mom had so many opportunities to forge a relationship with you; Gertrude did as well. If only they could have made more of an effort, or at least tried to put themselves in your shoes. Your mom could have taken you to the movies herself and out for a meal afterward. It would have been such an easy thing to do, such a simple gesture that could have brought you closer together.

After Daddy's death, you and I started going to the movies often. It was one of my favorite things to do with you, and I looked forward to it all week. I liked sitting in a darkened theater together, sharing popcorn, waiting for the film to begin.

ANDERSON COOPER and
Gloria Vanderbilt

It reminded me of when my father would sometimes take me out after dinner for a slice of pizza around the corner from our house on Sixty-Seventh Street. It wasn't that I was hungry, but it was an opportunity for the two of us to spend time together. To this day, whenever I smell pizza, I think of sitting with him at a linoleum table, talking about what happened that day in school or whatever else was on my mind.

I'm sorry you didn't get to have that kind of interaction with your mother, or with Gertrude.

Some people really should not be parents, and perhaps my mother was one of them. To have a child, you have to be able to extend yourself, and she wasn't capable of that. The only person she could truly love was her identical twin sister, Thelma.

She once told me, "When you were born, you were so tiny I was afraid to hold you."

We just never connected. She was too young and self-involved to bond with an infant. By the time I was an adult, it was too late.

I remember I was visiting her one weekend in New York and I was brought into her room to say hello. She sat at her dressing table as Wannsie, her lady's maid, brushed her hair.

Looking straight at me in the mirror as I stood behind her, she said, "How about dyeing my hair blond?"

Was she joking? It didn't sound so, because her voice—with its hesitant stammer, usually so soft one almost had to lean in close to hear what she was saying—was different now, threatening even.

"Don't *do* that, Mummy," I wanted to scream, but of course I didn't. Meekly I stood silent, transfixed, while Wannsie continued brushing the dark hair rippling down to my mother's waist before combing it into a middle part with gentle waves on either side of her face, then twisting it back to secure into a cushiony pillow of a chignon.

"Run along now," my mother said, "let me finish dressing." I ran out the door of her room crying, but unsure why.

My mother had started dating A. C. Blumenthal, who was a very wealthy real estate investor and theater promoter. He would send his driver to pick up Tootsie Eleanor and me at the movie theater and take us back to her house on Seventy-Second Street, between Park and Madison. When we returned, my mother would be sitting in the living room smoking a cigarette, the inevitable pale drink on the coffee table in front of her.

"Did you have a good time, darling?" she'd ask. I'd sit beside her on the sofa, and she would struggle to think of other topics of conversation. I wasn't much help. But the time would pass, and soon the moment would come for Freddy to drive us back to Old Westbury.

And Auntie Ger. Why was I always the one who reached out to hug her before she would embrace me? She was so reserved and always polite, but she brilliantly edited herself. In all the years I lived with her, we never spoke about my father, her own brother, and my mother's name was never spoken between us. Of course now I realize how cautious she had to be after the custody trial. She couldn't say anything derogatory about my mother that might be seen to make me more fearful of her than I already was. But even without talking about my mother or father, they were there, no matter where I went, unknowable, ghostly, and strange.

Sometimes it was difficult to keep the ball rolling in conversations with Auntie Ger, but in those moments, she would reach over to the coffee table in front of the sofa and pick up the latest copy of *House and Garden* magazine. "Let's look at the rooms," she'd say, opening to a page. "What do you think of this decoration?"

I had no problem expressing my opinion when we discussed this or that room. It was fun, and I felt at ease with her as never before. My heart soared when she was interested in hearing my opinion.

Eventually, when I understood what my aunt had been up against, I came to love her, but I was an adult by then, and she was long gone. She died shortly after I turned eighteen.

I know you started painting when you were ten. Were you influenced at all by the fact Gertrude was an accomplished sculptor and art collector? Did she have a creative influence on you?

I wish I could say that she was an influence on my artistic development, but the truth is, she never talked about art with me. The only time she mentioned her sculpture in my presence was when I was fifteen and she permitted Louise Dahl-Wolfe to come to Old Westbury to photograph me for *Harper's Bazaar*. Auntie Ger made it clear to Wolfe and her team that no photographs were to be taken of me with her sculpture *Diana*, which was prominently placed in the center of the courtyard in front of her house. She was after all a serious artist and didn't want her work appearing in a fashion magazine.

There had been many times during the years I lived with her that I longed to talk with Auntie Ger about her art, but I didn't dare bring it up. I was afraid, too, of telling her how often I had walked around alone in her darkened studio, removing the coverings from her sculptures and gazing in wonder, longing to ask questions, talk to her. But I never did.

So what did influence me to become an artist? It was not only something I wanted to be; it was something I could not stop myself from becoming.

Before me is a small painting of a dancing girl in a pink dress. Her thin arms out wide, she appears to be in midflight. It is the first oil painting I did, at age ten, while attending the Greenvale School.

On the table below this painting is a sculpture I made from clay, also at Greenvale. It is of a girl leaning against a rock, her face hidden in her arms because she does not want to reveal she is crying. Yes, sobbing because she is desperate, so distraught she contemplates killing herself.

Everywhere I have lived over the years, I have always displayed these two early works of mine, which tell of the turmoil that raged within me after the custody battle. There were moments when I was the dancing girl—joyous, full of hope. Those feelings were real, but so were the feelings of the girl sobbing her guts out, tears flowing unseen as she hides her head in shame. Is it her fault her father was an alcoholic and her mother a lesbian? Would she also grow up to be one or the other, or perhaps both?

Is this what led to the spells of drinking and sobbing that began in my twenties? Spells long since abolished? Did the dancing girl in the pink dress push the girl on the rock away so that she no longer existed?

Is this how and why I became an artist? It was early on in those days at Greenvale that I started painting, and I've kept on doing it ever since and will until the day I die.

In my late teens I became a student of Robert Beverly Hale and John Carroll at the Art Students League in New York. Mesmerized as I was by the ethereal beauty of Carroll's work, I was thrilled when he asked me to model for him.

Today, that first Carroll portrait hangs in my living room. In it, a passive girl in a gold Fortuny dress gazes out, but she is a stranger to me now.

If she'd only known then what I know now, but she remains as she was, unaware that one day she will meet your father, and that he will die long before she does. She has no idea she will launch a successful career in home furnishings and fashion and become a painter and a writer, and that one day she will stand on a balcony pleading with her son Carter not to let go of the ledge he clings to fourteen floors above the East River.

What do I wish I'd had when I was growing up? A mother and a father—parents I could depend on from the beginning, balanced and sure of heart. Parents I could talk to about my hopes and dreams. Parents to make me aware I had choices.

It's always interested me how some people are able to propel themselves forward no matter what happens while others are hobbled or done in by their circumstances. Where do that drive and determination come from? Are they something you are born with or do you develop them based on experience?

Had you not faced the traumatic events of your childhood, would you have been so driven? Would you have accomplished all that you have? I ask this of myself as well.

If my dad hadn't died and Carter had not killed himself right before my senior year of college, if I hadn't been left reeling by those losses, would I have taken the risks I did early on in my life and my career? I don't think so.

Both their deaths changed me in ways I am only now becoming aware of. I didn't realize it at the time, but it was because I was grieving after Carter's death, and worried about my own survival, that I felt compelled to go to places where there was suffering and loss, where the pain outside would match the pain I was feeling inside. I wasn't sure I could survive, and I wanted to learn from others how they were surviving.

I hadn't applied for any jobs my senior year of college because I felt so confused after Carter's death. Once school was finished, and I'd taken some time to travel, I asked a friend to make me a fake press pass so I could go to war zones with a camera to shoot stories, but I didn't know that it would lead to a lifelong career. It was just something I felt I had to do.

My drive certainly comes from the experiences I had early on, the fear, and all the other feelings that built up in me as a child. Because I had the same name as my mother, as an adult it became of utmost importance to me to work under the name I was born with. Although I have never told you or any one else, I did this because I believed that if I succeeded in writing, or acting, or painting, it would expiate in some mysterious and secret way the public vilification of my mother and free her to love me as I longed to be loved. Can you understand this? My wish, though fervent, was like water passing through a sieve, but it continued throughout my life, and in many ways still does.

Something else that motivated me early on was an article I accidentally saw during the custody case, in a copy of the *Daily News* that had been left in the kitchen in Old Westbury. There was a photo of me heading into court under the headline "Poor Little Rich Girl."

It was the first time I saw that phrase. I was stunned, confused. Was *that* who I was? I didn't feel "poor," and I didn't feel "rich." I felt like a ten-year-old girl with hopes and dreams who couldn't wait to grow up and find out what it would be like to be a *person*. I was being branded with word-play so catchy that it would stick. I was terrified it would be with me forever.

I did not want to be the "Poor Little Rich Girl," and it made me determined to make something of my life. I've never been able to admit how intensely it motivated me. I'm not even sure I should admit it now, but it no longer matters. I have achieved many of the things I wanted to in my life, and the sting is gone.

I remember an interviewer on a local news show in Chicago once said to me, "Why do you work so hard? If I were Gloria Vanderbilt, I would be on a beach somewhere."

That always stuck in my mind. It says more about the interviewer than it does about me. It should be everyone's right to nourish and develop the talents they have, and in so doing add their contribution to the world, however large or small. Why should someone born into a wealthy family be any different? None of us chooses the situation into which we are born. To think that if you are from a rich family you should not want to achieve something on your own is a foreign idea to me.

As for you, Anderson, you have always had a fierce drive, a burning desire to make a name for yourself. For a long time I don't think people even knew you were related to the Vanderbilt family.

T hat was intentional on my part. I didn't want to be burdened by other people's judgments and assumptions. I didn't want people to think I was just dabbling in journalism and/or that reporting was a hobby.

A lot of people probably believe that you don't have to work, either, but I've always been impressed that you've never let others define who you are or what you care about.

The first time you told me that you didn't read anything about yourself, I thought it strange, but now I understand why you don't. I'm guessing it was something you learned early on, after being written about in tabloids during the custody trial.

I did an experiment recently and stayed off Twitter for a weekend, and I was so much happier without reading strangers' comments about me. It's hard to calculate just how destructive other people's opinions can be.

Yes, I would hate that. I find the idea of Twitter fascinating, but I have no desire to join it. People revealing things they feel at the moment that can't ever be taken back—a lot of people are going to regret the things they've said.

The craving to be famous is like an insidious disease. No matter how well known you become, it's never enough; it never satisfies.

I have never let myself dwell on other people's opinions of me. Perhaps they thought I was dabbling in acting, painting, or writing, but it doesn't touch me. If that is what they think, so be it. You can never change their minds, so why waste time trying? Why agonize over it? Better to concentrate on more important things.

It has taken me a long time to figure that out. I try not to read what people write about me, but it's sometimes hard to ignore. Also I think it's important for me professionally to be open to criticism. I still have a lot to learn, and want to get better at what I do. I don't ever want to feel too comfortable in my career.

Well, I can certainly understand that, but I think there is a difference between being open to constructive criticism and letting jealous strangers say cruel things to you that make you feel bad about yourself.

As a child, I had to ignore what people said about me, or else I would have been done in. I would have turned into a pillar of salt. After the custody case and all throughout my teenage years, I was constantly pursued by the press.

The public had formed opinions about me and wanted updates about my life, and newspapers were only too happy to oblige.

I developed a survival tactic: I imagined I had a protective cloak over my shoulders that sheltered me from the storm. I used this often, like when I was thirteen and being confirmed, and photographers followed me up to the altar in the church.

I know that my father was raised Baptist, but what was your religious background and what do you believe now?

My father's family was Episcopalian, and my mother's Catholic, so I was christened in both faiths. I had no religious instruction until Surrogate Foley, who still had responsibility for me, decided I was to be raised Catholic and should have religious training. Every Friday after school, I was sent for instruction with Father Fealey. I adored him. He always had a little bowl with square, crunchy white mints on a table, and I'd eat them while he rambled on and on. I took it very seriously, but the way he presented things, the horrors of the Crucifixion didn't sound so bad. Mary Magdalene was the star, as far as I was concerned—naughty and beautiful. What better combination?

I became extremely caught up in it all and decided to be a nun when I grew up. That all changed of course, once boys came into the picture.

My First Holy Communion was a private ceremony in Old Westbury, with no family present. I have to admit I really hadn't a clue about what was going on, but I did feel a sudden mystical something. Dressed as I was like a bride, in white with a veil, I imagined this was what it must feel like to get married.

The next week, I was confirmed with a large group of girls at another parish, dodging paparazzi as we edged slowly toward the altar. Required to take saints' names, I chose Regina, in memory of my father, and Francesca because I loved the name. One of the girls in the long line was chattering about what her mom had planned for dinner after the service. I boasted about the mix of delicacies my mom was preparing. Of course, I made it all up.

I still remember the thrill of the confessional! I tremble reliving the awe, the mystery, as I waited to enter the dark cave: the slight "woosh" as I opened the velvet curtain separating me from the priest.

"Bless me, Father, for I have sinned."

There were times when I was hard-pressed to come up with a sin. It's not that I was perfect, but my mind often went blank. I knew it was wrong to receive Holy Communion unless I had gone to confession first, so often I just made something up, letting my imagination run wild.

It was so dark inside that I was never certain if it was Father

Fealey or someone else to whom I was confessing. Whoever it was listened silently and then offered brief counsel before pronouncing, "Five Our Fathers, and fifteen Hail Marys," or whatever. Clutching my rosary beads, I'd scurry out to kneel in front of the altar.

Soon after my confirmation, I was taken by Auntie Ger and Naney to have tea with Cardinal Spellman at his private quarters in St. Patrick's Cathedral. I felt paralyzed as the three of us sat in the gray Rolls-Royce on our way there, and I felt that way all during the tea party, except when I curtsied meeting the cardinal.

Naney, on the other hand, continued her chatter about our kinship to Saint Ignatius of Loyola, while Auntie Ger, very much at ease, skillfully moved the conversation to more recent topics, graciously trying to involve me by mentioning my activities at Greenvale.

It was as if we were in a play, sitting in that quiet room in the presence of Cardinal Spellman, the horns of taxis and traffic outside muffled to silence by His Eminence.

For an instant, Auntie Ger appeared to me as Saint Gertrude and Naney was Saint Naney Napoléon. As for me? Saint Francesca Regina, of course. Why not? The image lasted only a blink, but last it did.

In the car on our way back to Old Westbury, I longed to confide my illuminating apparition to Auntie Ger and Naney, but decided it was too risky. Anyway, Naney was so energized by the experience that even Auntie Ger couldn't get a word in as she chitchatted away.

I no longer attend Mass, but there are times even now when I sense a mist covering that which I gaze on. If I could only penetrate this mist, it would reveal a place I know well.

What am I if no longer an ardent Catholic? An agnostic, I suppose, but I do believe in a mysterious force secretly in charge of our destiny, enabling us to make life bearable and keep moving even when times are tough. The end will turn out as it was always meant to be. Yes, from the beginning, we have nothing to do but wait.

Our choices are preset from the beginning. Whatever direction a person's life goes in was destined. It was meant to happen in precisely that way, although we do not as yet know why.

I don't believe that the end will turn out as it was always meant to and that all we have to do is wait, and I'm not sure you do, either. That sounds like magical thinking.

Everything is predestined? Come on. You have worked relentlessly to give shape to your life, as have I. What about all those people for whom things do not work out? Was it just not meant to be for them?

I don't mean that it is going to end up well for me or for anyone else. But I do believe if it doesn't end well, then there is a reason for that. It's like finding a piece of a puzzle that completes a picture. Things happen as they are meant to, for better or for worse.

You really believe that things always happen as they are meant to? I don't think that's true. What about accidents? Disasters? Children who die young because they don't have access to clean water or antibiotics? I don't think there is a reason those children die. It is senseless death and unfair, not somehow predestined or meant to be. We will just have to agree to disagree on this topic.

Three

After the custody trial was over, my grandmother continued to live in New York and received a regular, though reduced, income from my mother's trust fund. In addition to supervised visits on weekends, the court also mandated that my mother spend several weeks with her mother each summer.

The summer after I was confirmed, my mother announced that we were going to go on a brief trip. It was the first time since the custody case that Surrogate Foley, my guardian, permitted her to take me out of New York State. She told me we were going to visit Hollywood.

"Wouldn't it be fun to meet some of my friends?" she asked.

It certainly would! I knew she was talking about movie stars, and I couldn't believe it!

The train trip lasted three days but seemed like forever.

Side by side, Tootsie Eleanor and I sat gazing out at the landscape speeding by. I kept singing out, "Hooray for Hollywood, that screwy, ballyhooey, Hollywood . . ."

But I did this only when my mother was in the compartment adjoining ours. I didn't want her to think I was behaving foolishly, and my voice, wild with excitement, tended to wiggle off-key.

Actually, we saw my mother only now and then. She liked to sleep late, and Wannsie brought her breakfast and lunch on a tray. She would join us at dinner, in the dining car.

We got off the train in Albuquerque for a few minutes, and my mother mingled on the platform with Native Americans in feathered headdresses selling handmade silver and turquoise jewelry.

When she got back on and went into her tiny compartment, she found a huge basket of white peonies with a note attached. For an instant she looked happy, but when she opened the card, her expression soon faded.

"From Maurice . . . how sweet," she sighed turning away to look out the window at a man holding up a turquoise necklace to get her attention. Maurice Chalom was a very successful French decorator with whom she was involved on and off for several years.

When we arrived in Los Angeles, we ensconced ourselves at the Ambassador Hotel.

My mother had made all sorts of plans. The first was to visit the actress Constance Bennett. She had hired a driver and a Rolls-Royce to take us around during our stay, and we drove to Beverly Hills, where Bennett lived with the actor Gilbert Roland.

To set foot in their house was to enter a beige-on-beige world: carpeting, furniture, curtains—all different shades of beige. A butler let us in as, side by side, down the winding staircase, descended a gorgeous beige couple.

Bennett wore a long, clinging beige dress. Her softly sculpted beige-blonde hair was coiffed back over her ears, which were clipped with topaz earrings. My mother later re-marked admiringly, "She was so thin, if she ate an olive it would show."

Gilbert Roland wore a beige shirt and slacks with a scarf casually placed around his neck, accenting his handsome face and black, black hair. It was a riveting moment, at least for me!

My mother, ever at ease, was greeted with hugs and kisses, while I sat goggle-eyed, listening to gossip about this and that Hollywood star.

Next stop was the hospital, to see Maureen O'Sullivan, who was recuperating from giving birth to a daughter. I had seen all her movies co-starring Johnny Weissmuller and was stunned that I was now actually sitting in a chair by her bed.

"Is it all right to speak in front of . . ." Maureen whispered to my mother while nodding to me.

"Oh, yes," my mother assured her, subtly shaking her head. I think she meant talking about giving birth. Of course I was dying to hear more, but they didn't pursue the conversation, so I didn't get any details.

The next night, my mother took me to a party at the Trocadero, on Sunset Boulevard, though she told me I could stay only for a little while, because it was for grown-ups and would continue late into the night. Speechless, I sat with her at a table next to Dolores del Rio, with Loretta Young across from us.

The room was filled with movie stars I had seen only on the silver screen, in dark theaters, but here I was now, sitting with them in real life. And don't think I wasn't aware that my mother could hold her own among all that glamour and beauty! As for fatso me—well, there was still time to shed weight, wasn't there? Fiercely, I would put my mind to it. My heart beat faster as I vowed to achieve this goal, my spirits soaring as I glanced around the candlelit room, gulping it all in. I knew I would soon have to leave and get back into the car parked outside, where Tootsie Eleanor sat waiting to take me back to the Ambassador Hotel.

I was so excited that night I didn't sleep, going over and over in my mind all I had seen.

A few days later, my mother took me once again to Beverly Hills. "A really big surprise," she promised, but what could it be? The car stopped outside a house on Rodeo Drive, and she told me it belonged to Marlene Dietrich and that she was expecting us!

As the chauffeur opened the door, my mother said, "You wait here, Pooks, while I go in for a minute."

Pooks was a name she occasionally called me when in a good mood. I was beside myself—I was going to meet the most mysterious, glamorous, ravishingly beautiful of all movie stars.

In a drawer in my room at Old Westbury, hidden from everyone (especially Auntie Ger), I kept a twelve-by-fourteen-inch photograph of Dietrich that my mother had asked her to autograph especially for me. And now here I was outside the door of Dietrich's house about to meet her! Heaven can wait. "This is it," I thought as I twiddled my thumbs in anticipation.

But my mother didn't appear. Why was it taking so long?

"What time is it?" I asked the driver.

I knew it must have been at least an hour since she had entered the house. I started getting worried. Maybe something had happened to her?

Finally she came back to the car, and instead of taking me out, she got in beside me and told the driver to take us to back to the Ambassador. "Sorry, but Marlene wasn't feeling well. You'll just have to meet her some other time," she told me. And that was that. We drove back in silence.

Years later, when I was married to Sidney Lumet, he and I went to Marlene's New York apartment for dinner. She greeted us at the door wearing very little makeup and a nurse's uniform with white flat-heel shoes. The only other guest was Ernest Hemingway, who had known my half-sister, Cathleen, in Havana. Sidney and I sat in the living room talking with him while Marlene occupied herself in the kitchen preparing dinner. Now and again she would pop in to join the lively conversation.

It was the first time I had met her, and it seemed surreal indeed. The four of us sat cozily around the table, talking and eating, enjoying the excellent dinner she had cooked, but as far as I was concerned, there was a fifth guest present: my mother.

One Sunday on that Hollywood trip, we had lunch with Maureen O'Sullivan (who was now home from the hospital) and her husband, the director John Farrow. At one point he nodded toward me, whispering to my mother, "She has 'it.' "

I wasn't sure what he meant, but I'd read enough movie magazines to know that Clara Bow had "it," so "it" must be something fantastic. I spent a lot of time that summer staring at myself in the mirror trying to figure out what he'd seen.

Desperate to be bone-thin like Constance Bennett, or as slim as my beautiful mother, I worried the time away, preoccupied with the belief I would be forever encased in blubber. Eventually, I came to the conclusion that I should trust in God and make the best of whatever was bestowed on me. Even if I didn't turn out to be as beautiful as my mother, I was what I was, and I became determined to make it work. I would look in the mirror and think, "This is what I am, make the most of it. Trust it. Believe in it. Confidence will prevail!"

———

In the summer of 1941, before her senior year in high school, my mom was invited by her mother to visit her in Los Angeles. Gloria Morgan Vanderbilt had moved out of New York and was then living with her twin sister, Thelma, in a house in Beverly Hills.

My mother was supposed to stay in California for only two weeks, but when she got there she found herself un-supervised for the first time and decided she didn't want to return to her aunt and the restricted life she had known in Old Westbury.

———

It pains me to recall the events of that summer. I should never have been permitted to visit my mother in Los Angeles when I was seventeen. What a tragic error it was. I cringe at the terrible mistakes I made, the foolish choices. If I hadn't gone, I would have graduated from high school in 1942. I might have applied to college, or art school, which is what I really wanted to do.

Surrogate Foley approved a two-week trip for me to see my mother, as long as I was accompanied by a chaperone.

What Foley didn't know was that the chaperone, whose name was Constance, would be chaperoning from a distance, because she wasn't given a room at my mother's house. She was sent to a hotel, and there she stayed for a few days alone, without seeing me, until my mother told her she was no longer needed and then—*poof!*—off she went, back to New York. I never set eyes on her again, and though Auntie Ger was dismayed by the turn of events, there was nothing she could do about it.

It was sheer heaven at first. The day I arrived, I had lunch with my mother and Thelma on the patio of their house on Maple Drive. Thelma, who had divorced Lord Furness, was having an affair with a handsome actor named Edmund Lowe.

My magical mother sat beside me as Wannsie brought out a platter of smoked salmon. We sat under an umbrella filtering the sun, fleeting shadows gently altering the faces of my mother and her twin. I listened as they gossiped about their friends, this and that movie star. I was so happy. Why had I ever been afraid of her? Why had we been separated for so long?

But that lunch turned out to be the last.

A few days later a woman named Kitty Kelly suddenly appeared. She was an actress who had started her career in the Ziegfeld Follies and had minor roles in Hollywood in the 1930s and '40s.

From the minute I saw them together, I sensed something was going on. My passive mother was clearly enchanted by Kitty's extroverted, brassy personality. They shared secret jokes, and giggled a lot together, acting more like lovers than friends. Her behavior with Kitty confirmed that the testimony during the custody trial about her being a lesbian was true. This shocked me. I once again panicked that I was going to grow up and be like "that," too.

My mother would go to Kitty's house, disappearing for days. They called me from there once, waking me up in the middle of the night, both drunk, each taking turns grabbing the phone from the other, saying they had heard I was "smoking marijuana." I didn't even know what that was.

I hung up and lay alone in the darkness of my room, scared to death.

Aunt Thelma, who spent days locked in her room with Edmund Lowe, was at her wit's end and asked me, "What am I going to do about your mother?"

I had no answer. My mother and I had no beginning together, no previous history of intimacy to bond us. Maybe she was as scared of me as I was of her?

Living with her and Thelma in that house was like staying at a hotel with strangers doing their best to avoid each other. I came and went as I pleased. My mother had no interest in what I was up to.

It's only now that I realize she was trying to lure me away from Auntie Ger by permitting me to do anything I wanted. And it worked. In my confused mind, Auntie Ger became the Wicked Witch waiting to steal my newfound freedom even though I was not equipped to handle it and was scared to death of it, too.

I was like a bird let out of a cage, but soon after the first rush of freedom came the realization that there was no nest to return to. Each direction I flew toward drew me deeper into a dark land of confusion. And my two-week visit was turning into months. Auntie Ger was expecting me back in New York, where the chaperone, Constance, was waiting; my senior year in high school would start in September, but the thought of going back was inconceivable. The girl I had been in New York no longer existed.

Then, suddenly, Kitty was out of the picture, and my mother and Thelma never mentioned her name again. What had happened? I didn't ask. After that, my mother was around a little more, though I still saw her rarely.

When I did catch a glimpse of her on my way here or there, she would call out from the sofa in the living room, drinking a scotch and soda, "Have a good time, Pooks."

The one time I tried connecting with her was a failure. She slept in an oversize bed, and one night I asked if I could sleep in her room with her. She consented, and I lay at the edge of one side of the bed, while she lay on the edge of the other.

I couldn't think of anything to say; nor could she apparently. Silently we lay on opposite sides, on our backs, facing the dark ceiling.

"Goodnight, Mummy," I finally said.

"Goodnight, darling," she answered, rigid in the dark.

A surge of passionate love shot through me. I longed to pull her toward me, merge with her. I started to turn and reach out my arms, but as I did, I heard a soft sound coming from the little radio on the night table by her bed.

Unnoticed by me, she must have switched it on. A commercial jingled merrily,

Good evening, Friends
We recommend Blue Plate Number Two
Our food is the best in the whole wide West
What can we do for you?

By the light from the radio, I could tell she was already asleep.

You said you felt like a bird let out of a cage that summer. What were you doing with all that freedom?

ANDERSON COOPER and

Gloria Vanderbilt

Every night, I went out on dates with movie stars. To attract my attention, they had to be famous and much older: Errol Flynn, George Montgomery, Ray Milland, Van Heflin, Bruce Cabot, Edward Ashley. It was thrilling at first, but these men were the wolves of Hollywood, and it quickly became harmful.

Errol Flynn? You dated Robin Hood when you were seventeen?

I remember, when I was a kid, we'd watch old movies together and I'd sometimes ask you if you knew one of the actors in it.

"Oh, yes . . . ," you'd say, and though you never went into details, the silence that followed was always loaded with meaning.

I can see why it would have been exciting, but I can't believe your mother didn't try to stop you or at least urge you to be careful. As you said, these guys were wolves, and after being so sheltered, there is no way you could have been ready to take care of yourself around them.

It was totally inappropriate, not to mention dangerous. Every Saturday night I went out to Mocambo or

Ciro's. Wannsie would throw a huge fistful of Elizabeth Arden bubble bath into my tub and turn the water on full force, so that the bubbles leaped up into billows of scented, fluffy, white snow.

"And what will you be wearing tonight, Miss Gloria?" she would ask.

"The new Howard Greer, the one with the sequins that just arrived. The one like Rita Hayworth was wearing. Greer copied it for me, well, sort of . . ."

Wannsie would open my closet and spread the dress out on the bed as I sank into the warm bubbles. She would bring me one of my father's monogramed silver cocktail goblets, visibly frosted from the iced Dry Sack Sherry in it. Shivering, I would lean into the bubbles for the first sip. Did my mother know I was drinking alcohol? I wonder now. Had it ever occurred to her that I was seventeen and not of legal drinking age?

"Wannsie, put 'Elmer's Tune' on the phonograph, please."

As the Andrews Sisters' voices filled the room, I sang along,

What makes a lady of eighty go out on the loose?
Why does a gander meander in search of a goose?

Rising from the bubbles, I'd ring for Wannsie to please bring me another sherry, and she'd place it on my dressing table to sip as I gazed in the mirror deciding what makeup to apply for the evening ahead.

I'd sprinkle handfuls of Schiaparelli's perfume over my body. It was called Shocking de Schiaparelli and came in a bottle shaped like a female torso. It had become my signature scent because of the name. Yes, shocking, that is what I wanted to be. Not a silly seventeen-year-old who didn't have a clue which road to take.

These Saturday night rituals took hours, but the results rarely met my expectations. I never lost hope that my mother would be around so she would see me all dressed up and I'd get her approval. Maybe she'd even say I was pretty, but she never did, because she was never there.

"Welcome home," the smiling doorman would say, ushering me into Mocambo. Heads would turn as I entered with one movie star or another and the maître d' escorted us to a front-row table, the band blasting swingy tunes as couples danced cheek to cheek. How gorgeous they were! Could I pass muster with any of the stars seated at the tables around the dance floor? Fat chance! I didn't really belong, but I was there, wasn't I? At the time, I thought that counted for something.

It is hard for me to believe that my mother condoned such behavior. I certainly would never have let a child of mine run wild as I did that summer of 1941.

I keep seeing parallels between us that I never knew existed: similar impulses and ways of dealing with things.

I have a Polaroid of you and me that I keep on my desk at work. It was taken in 1985, when I was seventeen, on the day I was leaving home for Africa for six months. Eager for adventure, and wanting to get away, I had decided to leave high school in the middle of my senior year and ride across sub-Saharan Africa in a truck.

It's obviously not the same as running wild in Hollywood and dating movie stars, but the desire to be grown-up and on my own was similar. I was more focused than you at that age, more responsible. I had applied to college already, but didn't see any point in spending the last semester of high school at home in New York. I convinced my school it would be an educational experience to travel from South Africa to the Central African Republic, camping out every night along the way. It certainly was a learning experience, but I am surprised my school agreed. It never occurred to me that you might not let me go.

You were nervous and sad about my decision, but in the photo, you are standing next to me smiling.

You handed me a note and told me to read it on my way to the airport. I still have it today.

Darling Anderson,

I want you to know that I am in fine shape from every point of view and will continue to be so and that you must not worry about me.

I also want you to know that since the moment I set eyes on you—you have brought me nothing but Joy—and I will remember everything about you forever. Have a marvelous time.

—*Mom.*

Though you never tried to talk me out of leaving, it must have been difficult for you to let me go so far away for so long. Daddy had died seven years before, and Carter was already at college, so I was leaving you all alone.

I suppose you knew Africa was a place I had been reading about since I was a child and had developed a passionate interest in. When we lived near the United Nations for several years, I became fascinated by all the different flags that flew outside the General Assembly building. I was particularly interested in the flag of Zaire. It was light green with a large yellow circle in the center and a man's fist clutching a burning torch. The fist was said to belong to the dictator Mobutu Sese Seko. I had read a lot about Zaire and the brutal rule of Mobutu, and the idea of actually being able to go there seemed like an amazing opportunity.

Had I not gone on that trip, my life would have taken a very different path. Spending those months in Africa gave me confidence, and when I later decided to start going to war zones to shoot stories, I knew I could return to Africa and manage on my own.

In the years since, you've had to say good-bye to me an awful lot. I can't even remember how many times I've called you on the way to the airport trying to figure out the best way to tell you I'm flying to some dangerous place.

"Hey, Mom, I'm sorry to call you last minute, but I'm heading to Afghanistan for a little bit."

"Oh, you are? . . . Okay," you'll say.

I can hear the fear and concern in your voice, but you never ask me not to go.

"Just please be careful" is all you say.

I wrote you that note so you would not worry about me. The truth is, I was terrified that you were going, but it was important to you. Although you were very young, I knew you were smart and could take care of yourself, so I trusted you would be okay.

When I was seventeen, though, I really had no idea what I was doing. I plunged forward, desperate to reinvent myself overnight from an insecure teenager into a glamorous grown-up, but I had no compass and wandered down each new path only to find myself more bewildered and lost than I was before.

You had been preparing yourself for years to be on your own and had always been so independent. At some point you have to let your children go, make choices on their own, and be themselves.

Had you been running around with movie stars and staying out all night, I would have responded differently, but I never worried about you as a teenager, so I didn't feel like I had to watch over you.

On the other hand, I desperately needed someone to watch over me at seventeen. That was the summer I made one of the biggest mistakes of my life.

While I was having lunch at the Beverly Hills Hotel with a friend, I met a man named Pat DeCicco. He just came up and introduced himself. He sort of worked for Howard Hughes, but as far as I could make out, he was mostly a gambler and lived off the money he made playing gin rummy. Years later I came across a newspaper article describing him as an agent and a movie producer, as well as an alleged mobster working with Charles "Lucky" Luciano. Yikes!

When we met, I didn't know he was violent, and by the time I found out, it was too late. He fascinated me, as did the rumors surrounding him. He'd been married to the actress Thelma Todd, and after they divorced, she was found dead in her car in a garage. She had seen Pat the night before, at a party, and they had argued. There were rumors that maybe he killed her, though her death was determined to be either an accident or a suicide. The story captured my imagination, like something out of a novel.

W ait a minute. You started dating a guy who was a gambler and rumored to have killed someone? That's usually not the kind of information people put in their Tinder bio to attract dates. Didn't you think that was someone you should probably stay away from? Did you love him?

It had nothing to do with love. I was mesmerized, as if under a spell. I hadn't a clue about what I was doing, and no one ever took me aside and warned me. But you are right to be surprised.

Why would a seventeen-year-old girl, with so many other options and things to look forward to, not only become fascinated by, but quickly marry, Pat DeCicco, a thirty-three-year-old gambler with a dangerous reputation?

It has taken years to find the answer, but I go back to that quote by Mary Gordon: "Being fatherless leaves a woman with a taste for the fanatical . . . a fatherless girl can be satisfied only with the heroic, the desperate, the extreme."

Getting involved with Pat DeCicco was both fanatical and

an act of desperation. He was forceful, domineering, and supremely sure of himself. When you have low self-esteem, as I did, those qualities are attractive. He resembled Dean Martin—tall, dark, handsome, and extremely extroverted. Pat could have a roomful of people laughing in hysterics, though what he said wasn't really funny; the way he said it was. He would do anything to get a laugh and often used me as the punch line.

One day, soon after meeting DeCicco, I was on my way to see him and as I left my room, I saw my mother ahead of me on her way down the stairs. She hadn't noticed I was there. Her beautiful face, so often tense, appeared softer, almost as if she were happy. Her raven hair, not bound in a chignon, flowed loosely around the shoulders of a long silk Nile green dress I had never seen her wear before.

It was only a moment, but I stood watching her as she entered the living room below and sat on the sofa facing the portrait of her that my father had commissioned Dana Pond to paint when they were in Paris on their honeymoon.

"Wannsie, I'm expecting Mr. Hughes at six. Please show him into the living room," she called out.

I went down the stairs and headed toward the front door without speaking to her. As my hand touched the doorknob, the bell rang. I opened the door, and there, standing before me, was a very tall, very thin, very, very sensitive-looking man who made me weak in the knees.

And that is how I met Howard Hughes.

I quickly said, "Hello," but Wannsie was close behind, and as I hastened past Howard, she escorted him into the living room.

My mother was asleep when I got home that night, so I had to wait until late in the afternoon the next day, when she finally emerged from her room, to find out why Mr. Hughes had been there. Apparently he had come to speak to her about *me*. He wanted to give me a screen test.

"Of course, I told him it was out of the question," my mother said, sounding annoyed.

"Why? Why?" I cried out, "Why is it out of the question?"

"What makes you think you could ever be an actress?" she said, glancing over at me.

"I've often thought of it secretly, I have, I have!" I wanted to scream out. But I didn't.

Instead, I started dating Howard. Something had passed between us when I opened that door and saw him, and wild horses couldn't have prevented us from seeing each other again.

When my mother became aware of this, she seemed uninterested and never mentioned him again. Later, I learned she was angry because when Howard came to visit that first time, she thought he was coming to ask her out.

Early on in our relationship, I told Howard that Pat frightened me and was pressuring me, so he sent him off to Chicago to handle some minor job for Pan Am. It was a huge relief, but I was angry that I didn't have the courage to get Pat out of my life by myself.

W hen I think of Howard Hughes, I imagine him as a recluse living in the penthouse of the Desert Inn hotel in Las Vegas, using tissues to protect himself from germs.

I can't reconcile the man I dated with the man he apparently became. When I knew him, he was thirty-six, wildly romantic, and gentle, yet he had the power to rule the world.

I had never met anyone like him. He was extremely masculine, but there was a fragility about him, as if he were made of fine and tawny flesh; and a reticence, a shyness, which was extremely appealing after the crudeness of Pat.

When I was with Howard, I always felt that he was concentrating on me exclusively, and he was so easy to be with. Silences in our conversation were not empty spaces I wondered how to fill; they were as natural as breathing. It was as if we had known each other forever, yet whenever we got together, we plunged into wild joy as if it were our first meeting.

Howard was extremely possessive, and secretive about our relationship; no more nights dancing till dawn at Mocambo and Ciro's. He would pick me up at my mother's house in a shabby Oldsmobile and off we'd go. I never knew where. Often he would fly me in his plane to Catalina for dinner in a seaside restaurant. There were nights in his private screening room when he'd proudly show me films he produced and directed, *Hell's Angels*, with Jean Harlow, his first big success, among them. Some nights when he was working he'd ask me to wait for him in the screening room. I'd watch movies until he'd suddenly appear with a picnic dinner we'd prop on our laps and enjoy.

Best of all, sex not only worked, but it was the first time since I started having sex that summer that I didn't have to fake an orgasm.

Before long, though, Pat figured out why Howard had sent him to Chicago. He knew we were constantly together and started inundating me with phone calls.

"Smarten up, Fatsy-roo. He's never going to marry *you*!" he would shout.

I stopped listening, but began to wonder if perhaps he was right. In the moments we were apart, doubts took hold. Howard could have any woman in the world; how could I possibly compete?

Although with each meeting we grew closer, he never mentioned marriage. It didn't occur to me at that age that we needed to spend more time together before any serious plans could even be considered. We had only started seeing each other, but time had no meaning to me. I was frantic and impulsive. I was desperate to get away from my mother but determined not to return to high school and my previous life with Auntie Ger.

Suddenly, toward the end of summer, my legal guardian, Surrogate Foley, demanded that I return to New York immediately to meet with him. My senior year in high school was about to start, and he wanted to know why I wasn't there.

Howard would miss me, of that I was certain, but was he going to ask me to marry him? I didn't know. After all, we had only known each other for several months. My mother insisted on taking the next plane to New York with me. Howard alerted the pilot, who came to my seat and said Mr. Hughes had requested that he escort me into the cockpit, where I could watch them fly the gigantic jet.

Throughout the flight, I kept hearing Howard's voice in my head,

I love you, Gloria.

And my own: *Howard, I love you.*

To each other we said that. He meant it. So did I. There was no question in my mind that it was the truth. Everything was going to be all right.

But then we landed, and it wasn't. It turned out all wrong.

I did not go to Auntie Ger's house in Greenwich Village.

Instead, my mother checked us into the Hotel Marguery, on Park Avenue. In our suite, yellow roses, masses of them, brimmed over the rim of a crystal bowl. I rushed to open the card, knowing it was Howard who had sent them.

I did go and see my aunt, before the appointment with Surrogate Foley. I was happy to see her and put my arms around her as we sat on the sofa in front of the fireplace. I told her about Howard, boasting that we were planning to marry. She was pleased but cautious.

"I do think it wise to wait until you complete high school. See how you feel about it then."

Of course, it was a completely sensible suggestion, but then she threw me into a panic, saying, "Let's call him. You can introduce us on the phone."

Trembling, I went upstairs and dialed his number, imagining Auntie Ger congratulating us on our engagement. He answered immediately. We spoke briefly about how much we missed each other, but I made no mention of my aunt. I went back downstairs, where she was waiting.

"He's very busy right now, Auntie Ger. Maybe another time. . . ."

"Oh," she said pleasantly, but she seemed somewhat taken aback.

On my way back to the hotel, I kept clutching the religious medallion Dodo had sent me to give to Howard. I had written

her and told her we were in love. She'd had it engraved, G.V. TO
H.H. NOVEMBER 1941. Hesitant, I had not given it to him, and it
remains in my possession to this day.

Later that evening, I went to a party at the Pierre hotel, and
there he was—not Howard, but Pat DeCicco. He ignored me,
as if I weren't there. I, too, pretended I hadn't seen him, until
he came up to me looking angry and hostile.

"What is it with you!" he said, grabbing my arm.

I froze, a rabbit, terrified. He stared at me in silence. Then
pulled me toward him and said, "You're going to marry me."

I was repelled but fascinated by the darkness of his intensity.

What was the destructive force that drew me to him? Was
it my lack of self-esteem? Or something I dared not admit to
myself: that he treated me as I deserved to be treated, pun-
ishing me for having brought shame on my beautiful, beloved
mother by turning against her in the custody battle?

All I had to do was run back to the safety of life with my
aunt, but I didn't. The next day, I told my mother that Pat had
proposed. She was ecstatic, and hastily called the *New York
Times* to announce our engagement. Everything was happening too fast. Every time I thought of calling Howard, I panicked, and so I never did.

When I finally met with Surrogate Foley, Pat insisted on
being there. Foley controlled my trust fund and demanded
Pat sign a document stating he had no right to my inheri-

tance should we divorce. It was as if hot pepper had been sprayed in Pat's face. He jumped up, shouting abuse at Foley. It was an amazing performance. Head in my lap, I started to cry, but Pat dragged me from the room, leaving the document unsigned, and that was the last time I ever saw Foley.

"May you always be as happy as you are now," my mother kept simpering to me as she and Aunt Thelma bustled about, occupying themselves with wedding plans. It was like a weird Alice in Wonderland dream.

How had this happened?

Today I have plenty of theories, but there is really only one explanation: an immature seventeen-year-old girl was playing blind man's bluff in a dark forest. I felt unworthy to be loved by a man who treated me as Howard did, like a queen. Pat knew the secret of unworthy me. It's really no surprise that I soon found myself Mrs. Pasquale John DeCicco.

I t is a sign of how alone you were that no one sat you down and tried to help you make better choices.

I just looked up an old Movietone News newsreel of the wedding on YouTube. You and DeCicco are on steps outside the church. There are crowds of people watching, held back by police. The wind is blowing your veil, and the whole affair looks rushed and confused. There is one moment when you seem to laugh at something DeCicco says, but it looks like you're faking it. Your smile seems almost frozen.

Oh God, that wedding! It took place in Santa Barbara, at the Old Mission Catholic Church on December 28, 1941. It was a modest wedding, paid for by the allowance my mother was getting from Surrogate Foley.

I walked alone down the aisle in a dress designed by Howard Greer, with a thirty-foot veil trailing behind me. By tradition, it would have been appropriate for my mother's brother, my uncle Harry Morgan, to take my father's role in "giving the bride away," but he wanted nothing to do with the wedding. He and his children refused to associate with me, blaming me for rejecting my mother in the custody trial.

Dazed as a zombie on the altar, I stood, kneeled, stood, kneeled . . . while the four-hour High Mass droned on and on. Who was this stranger by my side, this tall, withdrawn dummy in a store window?

Then it was over. Two robots turned and walked back down the aisle and out onto the steps, where photographers and onlookers had gathered to view the proceedings. One newspaper noted, "The bride remained un-kissed." True, indeed.

ANDERSON COOPER and
Gloria Vanderbilt

The wedding party drove back to a cocktail reception hosted by my mother and Aunt Thelma, in their house on Maple Drive. Auntie Ger had been impressed when I told her about Howard Hughes, but she was very much against my marrying Pat, and there was no question of her attending the wedding, but Dodo and Naney were there, though they kept clear of my mother and Thelma. They enjoyed ogling the movie stars, and Dodo commented, "Rita Hayworth is the only one that looks aristocratic."

For our honeymoon, Pat's pal Bruce Cabot lent him a new car for us to drive to Kansas, so that Pat could begin his officer training course. It was just a few weeks after the attack on Pearl Harbor, and Pat had joined the army. Bruce's car was a sleek silver vehicle that appeared to come from a *Flash Gordon* comic strip. Pat got big laughs christening it "Flash Gordon's Bed Pan."

"Where are we spending our wedding night?" I asked as we drove off, waving to the assembled guests.

"A surprise," he responded.

It certainly was. After a few hours on the road, we stopped at Joe Schenck's house in Palm Springs. Schenck was chairman of 20th Century-Fox. Inside the home, Zeppo Marx and a group of men were playing cards. They briefly glanced up through the haze of cigar smoke to nod hello, indicating a room down the hall that was to be our bridal suite.

"Settle in," Pat told me. "I'll be back in a bit."

I lay in the dark waiting until 6:00 a.m., when he appeared for a quick . . . dare I say? . . . fuck. Then off we went for a breakfast hot dog and many more days on the road.

While Pat was in the army, I lived in a small rented house in Junction City, Kansas, for two years. I would see him on weekends, when he had leave. I didn't look forward to his arrival. He would constantly put me down, calling me Fatsyroo—and then there were his violent rages. He would scream at me and slap me.

I was so ashamed, and I didn't have anyone I could talk to about what was going on. I obviously shouldn't have made such a hasty decision to marry him, but my mother had moved so quickly to make it happen.

Auntie Ger had died four months after the wedding, which left me stunned. We hadn't spoken, because she was so opposed to my marrying Pat, and no one had told me she was even ill. I went to her funeral in New York, and in the car on the way back to my hotel, I completely collapsed, hysterical. I was so unhappy and miserable, and now I believed there was no one I could trust to help me out of this huge, awful mistake.

Though she was distant and reserved, your aunt had tried to bring a level of stability to your life that you had never experienced. I found a box of letters from her in storage last week and have sent them to you. She seemed to express things in writing that she never actually said to you in person, offering to "talk things over" with you and telling you how much she cared about you. In the letters, it was clear that she loved you and wanted to reach out to you. If only she had been able to express that to you when you were living with her all those years.

So many of the sweet words she wrote to me in letters when I was in Los Angeles that terrible summer were sentiments she had never been able to directly express to me. After you sent me that box of letters and I went through them, I wrote her a letter. It made me feel a little better, and perhaps somehow, somewhere, she will hear of it.

Dearest Auntie Ger,
There are some things I'd like you to know even though it's too late. I am sorry for the way I behaved at seventeen and I hope you know my actions came from bewilderment and panic. I felt alone and was unable to think clearly.

When your offer to "talk things over" finally came that summer I was staying with my mother in California, it was too late. If only we had been able to "talk things over" from the beginning, when I went to live with you in Old Westbury, my life might have taken a different turn. But that was not to be.

All this is to tell you how much I loved you and to thank you for rescuing me from the terrible fears I had concerning my mother. I wish we had come to know each other better—come closer, so to say, but this is tempered by peace in knowing we are closer in death than we ever were in life.

I'm sorry that I failed you, but I have to forgive myself because at the time I saw no other solution to resolve the confusion I was feeling. I like to believe you understand and in doing so forgive me as well, but more than anything else, I hope you know how much I love you and thank you for all you did for me—all you gave me.

Love,
Gloria

I wonder what would have happened if you hadn't married Pat DeCicco and had instead gone back to New York to live with Gertrude. She died in April 1942, so you would have been nearly finished with high school. Assuming you didn't marry Howard Hughes, you might have gone on to college or art school.

I think about that a lot, what might have been. Instead, I lived in Junction City for two years while Pat was stationed at Fort Riley. In 1942, on a quick trip to Washington, DC, we met Senator Happy Chandler. He seemed a happy fellow indeed, and if he wasn't, he certainly imitated one well. Pat and Happy really hit it off, both telling lots of jokes that I never found funny, though I would laugh along with them. Pat was soon calling him his new best friend, and together they were a merry Tweedledum and Tweedledee.

One evening, when I joined them at a restaurant in Washington, Pat told me that Happy had the clout to turn him from a first lieutenant into a captain if only we could come up with ten thousand dollars in cash to give him. Both Pat and Happy kept looking expectantly at me as we sat around the table.

Not yet twenty-one, I hadn't gained access to the money I was going to inherit, receiving a monthly allowance instead. Pat knew this, but when we got back to our hotel, he started shouting at me. "Sit your ass down and get Hughes on the phone. Tell him you need to borrow ten grand; you'll pay him back when you are twenty-one. And Fatsy-roo, don't be a dummy and tell him what it's for."

"I can't do that," I replied, and started to cry.

Pig-eyed with fury, he snatched the phone and shoved it into my chest.

Terrified, I called Howard, whom I hadn't spoken to since my engagement to Pat was announced.

When Howard picked up the phone, his only response was, "I thought you were calling to say you were coming back to me."

Howard and I never spoke again, and Pat did not get the undeserved promotion.

People stay in relationships for all kinds of reasons, but you did have options. You could have returned to your mother or moved back to New York. You had attorneys and a legal guardian, Surrogate James Foley, who controlled the money being held in a trust for you. Why didn't you leave DeCicco?

Oh, darling, why does anyone stay in an awful marriage? I knew I had made a horrendous mistake, but I didn't see an easy way out. I was an insecure eighteen-year-old who had never felt connected to her family, and I didn't think I had anywhere else to go. Auntie Ger wouldn't want me back after the way I behaved—or so I thought.

The first time I remember having a glimmer of belief in myself was when I was riding on a train back to Junction City after a visit to Los Angeles. In the seat across from me sat an older man, and next to him, his son. I was immersed in Jane Austen's *Pride and Prejudice* when suddenly I heard my name. I looked up from my book, but the men continued their conversation, clearly oblivious that the person they were gossiping about was sitting just an arm's length away.

"So sad, that Vanderbilt girl, just a kid from such a well-known family, with so much to look forward to. Why didn't someone do something to stop her from marrying a gigolo clearly after her money?"

My face stinging, I wanted to bolt out of the compartment and jump off the train, but I just sat there paralyzed.

"People say DeCicco murdered his first wife, that actress Thelma Todd. Wonder how he got Gloria to marry him. She's just a kid in her teens, and he's so much older, in his thirties."

I continued to sit with my head down in my book, as they chatted on—about my mother (saying hateful things) and Auntie Ger (who came out swell), but always returning to DeCicco and me.

"Surely she can only come to a bad end starting out like that."

Would I come to a bad end? It frightened me to hear it said out loud, so evident even to strangers.

We arrived in Junction City and stood in a long line slowly making our way off the train. Did I dare? Did I have the courage?

I tapped the older man on the shoulder and he turned around. "I'm Gloria Vanderbilt," I said.

He was speechless. His face dissolved in embarrassment and dismay; his son's as well. I thought they both might faint.

For me, though, there was a feeling of hope. I'd made a decision and had the guts to speak up for myself for the first time.

———

On the eve of being shipped overseas, Pat DeCicco came down with septicemia, which in those days was a life-threatening illness. He recovered but was discharged from the army. My mother finally left him in January 1945, after three years of marriage. She returned to New York one month before she turned twenty-one and inherited a trust that was then worth more than four million dollars.

———

Knowing I would soon receive my inheritance, I became more confident in myself, but what made me decide to leave Pat was that I got really scared of him. He would go into these dark rages, slapping and punching me. I finally told him I wanted a divorce, and left him shortly before my twenty-first birthday. His close confidant and gambling buddy Joe Schenck called me and said I could get a divorce if I paid Pat two hundred thousand dollars. There was no reason to give him anything. I could have easily gotten an annulment; but I wanted him out of my life fast.

"Okay, Joe," I said. And that was that.

When I turned twenty-one I started having a lot of fun. I was the girl of the moment. People were making a big fuss over me, and for the first time in years I was going out with friends my own age. The war was about to end, and it was an incredibly exciting time to be in New York. Not only that, but it was the year I inherited this wad of money from my father's estate, and as you might guess, I had no trouble spending it. The money meant I could take care of my beloved Naney and Dodo, whom I was able to see regularly once again, and I showered them with presents.

I also started supporting my mother financially. Despite her behavior the summer I lived with her in Los Angeles, and the hasty wedding she'd orchestrated, which had been a way for her to get back at Auntie Ger and protect her own financial future, I was drawn in again by her charm and beauty. I started to believe that maybe she did love me a little after all. I included her in the bounty bestowed upon me by the Vanderbilt money, giving her a hefty allowance and agreeing to her suggestion that we live together in an apartment on Park Avenue in New York.

By pushing you to marry Pat DeCicco, how was your mother getting back at Gertrude and protecting her own future?

If I was married under her auspices, it meant that I had sided with her, and no matter what the court had decreed in the custody trial, it made my mother feel like she had won in the end. She would get back at Gertrude by showing the world that she was in control of my life and that Gertrude no longer had any say in it. Also by connecting herself to me, she had a better chance of being able to get money from me.

One night I went to a party and met the conductor Leopold Stokowski. He appeared like a god. We were instantly attracted to each other, and it bowled me over to have this great genius suddenly madly in love with me. I couldn't wait to tell my mother. How proud she would be that this brilliant man was crazy about me and wanted to marry me.

But when I told her, she pulled back, flabbergasted and furious. It was the only time I ever saw her express anger.

"He's sixty-three! An old man!" she said, raising her voice. "You're just twenty-one. It's disgusting."

Did she honestly believe that, or did she know that if I married Leopold, the plans I'd recently made for her to live with me would no longer be possible? The lease on the apartment had already been signed and the place was ready for us to move into. She had envisioned herself romping around town, lunching at the Colony, or hosting little dinners *chez nous* with this or that whomever. Her social position would again be secure, while I danced the nights away at El Morocco or the Stork Club.

Of course, this didn't occur to me at the time. She agreed to meet Leopold only once, and the hatred on both sides was evident. She was not even influenced by the fact that Greta Garbo, whom she so admired, had had a long, serious love affair with him. He could have married Garbo, but instead he chose insignificant me. I was certainly impressed, but not my mother.

"It's *disgusting*!" she kept repeating after she had met him, her voice louder than I had ever heard it as it spun around the room. I was in tears after I left her, and stuttered as I tried to tell Leopold of my encounter with her and repeat the vile words she had said about him. He sat back in the chair, steady, calm, silent, sagely taking it all in, as I attempted to articulate the fears I'd had about her since the day I was born. But it was coming out tangled, too complicated to explain.

I kept on trying until he held up his hand, silencing me, then took me in his arms gently, quietly, with complete authority and simplicity, saying, "She *never* gave you love. It was Dodo who gave you love."

ANDERSON COOPER and
Gloria Vanderbilt

154

Of course, Leopold the god was right. Only he understood. From that moment on, passionately in love and under Leopold's spell, I cut my mother out of my life and left
her without a penny. I assuaged any guilt or doubts I felt by
telling myself that Thelma had a multimillion-dollar divorce
settlement from Lord Marmaduke Furness that she would
share with her, and they would live happily together ever
after.

From that day in 1945 until 1960, I did not see or talk to my
mother even once.

I didn't know you cut her out of your life. It's hard for me
to imagine you doing that, but you were a very different
person then. You were so passive in many ways, so easily influenced by others. DeCicco told you to marry him, and you
did. Then Stokowski wanted to marry you and have you cut
off your mother, and so you agreed.

At the risk of sounding like an armchair therapist, do
you think your attraction to a sixty-three-year-old man had
something to do with your wanting a father figure?

Oh, absolutely! But at the time, the fact that
he was so much older did not occur to me. I thought of him
as ageless. Of course, now I see it in a different light. Being
attracted to someone who was forty-three years older was

the act of a fatherless girl who was desperately seeking a dad, but back then, I didn't realize that, and I didn't understand my mother's reaction. I was astonished and bewildered. The indifference she had always had toward me had turned into hostility.

However, it all happened much, much too quickly. You can't spend just three weeks with a person and decide to get married, but that is exactly what I did. I met him in December, went to get my divorce in April, and we married in Reno on the day it became final.

There were moments when a voice inside my head would say, "Wait, wait! After years of DeCicco calling you Fatsy-roo and giving you black eyes, take some time to find out what you really want." But alas, these moments were fleeting. I should have remained unattached, and allowed myself to figure out who I really was, but Leopold's love was a force I couldn't resist. I was deeply in love as well, and flattered he wanted me to be his wife.

The first summer we were married, he was conducting at the Hollywood Bowl, so we moved to his house in Los Angeles. Then we moved to New York, into a penthouse apartment at 10 Gracie Square. That is where I got pregnant, first with Stan, then two years later with Chris.

You write that "it all happened too quickly," as though marrying him were beyond your control. I know you were insecure and young, but you had so many options. It obviously didn't feel like that to you at the time. I think back to when I was twenty-one and just graduating from college. I realize now I also had options, but I wasn't aware that I did. When I decided to start going to war zones to shoot stories, it felt like that was the only path I could take. I had to make that work. I had no plan B.

Given how low your self-esteem was, what was it like when you became a mother for the first time? You were twenty-six when you gave birth to Stan. Was motherhood what you thought it would be?

Being a mother wasn't what I expected at all. I was sure I would have a girl, and it was a shock not to; the second time, another shock, and then again and again. Little did I know that you, Carter, Stan, and Chris would be the greatest joys of my life.

Every time I've been pregnant I believed I was doing the most important thing in the world. But afterward, I really didn't know what to do. I wasn't relaxed and could never nurse for long. I felt tremendous guilt, as if there were something wrong with me.

I wanted to correct the mistakes my mother made with me, but I didn't know how. I read books on parenting, but none gave me the answers I was seeking. I fantasized about creating a large family, but my dreams were simplistic, and I kept reaching out blindly for some kind of road map to follow. I thought God Leopold could lead the way, but it turned out that, obsessed by his work, he knew as little about parenting as I did, though he had three other children by previous marriages. Also he wasn't around very often. He was touring constantly, and the choice was to either go around the world with him and two young children, which I didn't want to do, or try to create the home I desperately longed for.

Where I failed with Stan and Chris is that I didn't really talk to them about important things when they were growing up. No one had ever talked to me about anything, so I had no frame of reference. I expressed my love with hugs and affection, but rarely communicated with them about significant events occurring in our lives.

Leopold and I separated in 1954, after nine years of marriage. I remember asking Dr. McKinney, the psychiatrist I had started to see, "What should I say to Stan and Chris?"

"Tell them, 'I guess you boys have noticed your father and

I haven't been getting along lately, and we are going to sepa-rate,' " he replied.

Well, of course that was true, but it was hardly enough in-formation to give to young kids.

W hy did you decide to get a divorce from Stokowski?

Leopold was very possessive. He didn't want us to have any friends, or have a life beyond the two of us. At first it was romantic, but over the years, it wasn't easy. In retrospect, I see he was like this because he was prob-ably nervous that I would discover he'd invented his past.

Leopold had told me that he was an illegitimate child re-lated to a royal family and had been brought up in Poland. He claimed his mother died when he was a child, and he said he'd been raised by a governess, who sounded very much like Dodo. This made me feel close and connected to him, but none of it turned out to be true.

He grew up in England, with a brother and parents, and there had been no governess. Everything he had confided in me about himself was a lie. I had told him everything about myself, but he hadn't trusted me enough to tell me the truth. His real background wouldn't have made any difference to me, but the fact that he lied to me, deceiving me into loving a fan-tasy he'd created, did matter.

I began to discover his deception only when he took me to meet the woman he claimed was his governess. We were on a train to Bournemouth, where she was in a nursing home, and as he talked about her, I started to realize this woman really was his mother. That was the beginning of the end. He wasn't the god I had made him out to be.

But I really got the power to leave Stokowski only when I met Frank Sinatra. He was in New York playing at the Copacabana for a couple of weeks, and he asked Jule Stein to introduce us. That's when I moved out of our apartment and took the kids with me.

The divorce was very bitter. Leopold fought for custody of the children, which dragged on for more than a year. He didn't think I would be willing to go through a custody battle, given the trial I had experienced as a child, but he underestimated me. I was willing to fight, and I won. He was granted visitation rights.

With the passing of time, however, I now remember much that was magical about our relationship. No longer is he a monster who tried to take my children from me. He is, once again, the genius I first encountered. He and Howard Hughes were among the most extraordinary men I've ever known.

There was nobody like Leopold. He was supportive about my painting and other creative pursuits. He never put me down or spoke harshly to me, and that was a huge encouragement. He always built me up, making me feel that I was the most beautiful, extraordinary woman. I'd never had anyone do that for me except Howard Hughes, in our brief relationship. His great love for me helped my self-esteem enormously.

If I could rewrite the story of our marriage, I would, but the deeds are done. Nothing can be changed, only the memories shuffled, making it possible to forgive him and myself for what went wrong between us.

It is nice that you can look back on your relationship with him and see the positive things he did for you despite how it all ended. That certainly is a mark of maturity that many people are not capable of.

I love the pictures I've seen of you and Sinatra together. You look so beautiful and happy. What was Sinatra like?

Does one ever know what another person is really like, even someone very close to us? Do we know what we are like ourselves? What we are today may not be what we are tomorrow.

I can only tell you what he was like to me, first as a lover and later as a lifelong friend. As lover, he made me believe I was the most important person in the world to him. As a friend, I knew I could always depend on him.

Sinatra was a knight in shining armor who came and rescued me from Stokowski. I never expected that we would stay together for very long, and we didn't—only about three weeks—but it gave me a gigantic boost to suddenly have him in my life.

Of course, today I could rescue myself. I wouldn't need a knight to come along, but it has taken a lot of time to sort it out and come to that place.

I do think it curious you felt the need to be rescued by Sinatra or by any man. I've always felt I had to rescue myself, and not depand on anyone else to. I am not saying my way of thinking is better, but the idea of waiting for a knight in shining armor to come along is foreign to me.

I think men are something of a mystery to you. I remember when I was a teenager, and you were in a relationship with a man who was married. For years he kept telling you he was going to divorce his wife and move in with you. Every time you mentioned this to me, I thought it was obvious he was lying, and I assumed you knew but just didn't care.

I never told you what I thought about his empty promises until I realized you actually believed them. When I finally told you he wasn't being honest, you seemed genuinely surprised. After all the men you have known, you still don't understand them very well at all.

That's absolutely true.

Your father once said to me, "You respect and trust women more than you do men."

He was right. Could it be because I grew up without any men in my life? My mother's suitors came in and out of the house in Paris, escorting her to dinners and parties, but I never talked to them. I was told to curtsy, and say, "How do you do?" That was it.

Later, when I lived with Auntie Ger, there were no men I really knew. After my embarrassment when I asked her attorney, Frank Crocker, if he would be my father, even if an appropriate candidate for a father figure had come along, I doubt I would have risked another rejection. For much of my life, men seemed always just out of reach, unknowable. Like an octopus, I stretched out my tentacles, desperately hoping to latch on to someone floating by who would give me the stability I so sorely lacked. I always hoped and believed that if a man loved me, everything that was wrong in my life would be put right.

So many of my early beliefs about men were formed by the fairy tales Dodo occasionally read to me: Cinderella rescued by Prince Charming from her wicked stepsisters. I would fall asleep dreaming a prince was waiting out there somewhere; all I needed to do was grow up so we could move into his castle, where we would live happily ever after.

It is in my nature to be romantic, and for me that meant falling in love with someone strong, tall, and handsome; someone to look up to, who adored me, and who would take care of me while I doted on them.

Keep in mind, these ideas I'm revealing come from a time now past, but I held on to them far longer than I should have. Except for DeCicco, I have been blessed with great love, but after Leopold's betrayal, it was difficult for me once more to give a man all of myself.

It is only through knowing you, Carter, your father, and Sidney Lumet that I came to respect and trust men as I do women. I came to stand free and clear of crippling fears, the sobbing in the dark.

———

My mother was thirty-one when her divorce from Stokowski was finally granted, in 1955. By then she had already fallen in love with Sidney Lumet, a director working in theater and television, who would go on to direct a number of legendary films, such as 12 Angry

Men, Dog Day Afternoon, Serpico, *and* Network.
When my mother left Stokowski, she intended to take her
sons, Stan and Chris, and move to Los Angeles to pursue
acting, but after Sidney came into her life, she once again
changed her plans.

———

Richard Avedon introduced me to Sidney,
telling me, "You may have something to give—each to the
other." He was right. Instantly, Sidney and I fell in love, and
just three weeks later, he bought the wedding rings. I wasn't
sure I wanted to get married again, and I certainly didn't want
to that quickly.

At the time, I was in New York in a play called *The Swan*,
and Frank Sinatra had come to a rehearsal and asked me to
sign a contract with him to appear in three movies he was
producing. I was excited and signed the contracts, but Sidney,
wildly insecure, worried that if I went to Hollywood, I would
remain there and he would lose me, so eventually I asked Sinatra to release me from the contract. I stayed in New York and
started studying acting with Sanford Meisner at the Neighbor-
hood Playhouse.

There was always part of me that wanted to be a movie star,
but when I got involved with Sidney, I dismissed the idea. Had

I thought it through, I could have done at least one movie with Sinatra and seen what happened, but I didn't. Over time, I began to resent Sidney for the decision I had made.

Sidney was separated from his first wife when I met him, and after he went to Nevada and got his divorce, he quickly returned to New York. "Now we can get married," he said.

When I suggested, "Let's wait," he was devastated. I couldn't bear to hurt him, so I said yes.

It seems so clear now that you had no long-term plan, no sense of direction. You never sat down and really thought about what you wanted. You always allowed men you were involved with to make decisions for you.

That is true. I went with the flow, rarely having a plan or thinking seriously about the future. When I was in my early teens, I thought, "I want to get married and have a big family and wear an apron in the kitchen, cooking like the mother in the Andy Hardy movies." That was the kind of dream I wanted to make real. Later, I flirted with the idea of going to college or art school, but instead went to Los Angeles that summer, and all those ideas disappeared.

The future has never had much reality to me. It still doesn't.

I wish I had made plans, but that just didn't seem realistic to me. Even now, I think about death; I think about you, Stan, and Chris, and your futures, but I don't think about my own, the coming months or years.

I've always been way too impulsive for long-term plans. You and I are very different in this way.

That is for sure. I plan all the time, and I think it's because I grew up knowing you did not. I always sensed, after my father died, that there wasn't a plan, and it worried me tremendously.

I remember lying awake at night worrying about what I would do when I became an adult, what kind of career I would have, how I would support myself. I would try to figure out how much money I needed to earn to be able to take care of you and Carter and May.

I used to fantasize about having a board of directors I could go to for advice: wise men and women, pillars of the community who would offer me sage counsel. I still kind of like that idea, though I find it very difficult to actually ask anyone for advice or for help. It is something I have rarely ever done.

Throughout your life you have had lawyers and financial advisers, and they must have urged you to plan ahead, but

I'm guessing it just sounded like they were speaking a different language to you
   Why don't you plan ahead?

   It never occurred to me as a child that when I grew older I would have choices and could make plans. The first eight years of my life I had no permanent home. We traveled from one place to the next, in France, England, Switzerland, one hotel or house to another. Dodo and Naney were my only home. We three traveled around with our Vuitton trunks and suitcases, packing and unpacking, living in the moment.

   The only inkling about plans came to me filtered through gauzelike whisperings between Naney and Dodo.

   Even as a teenager my plans, such as they were, were all short term, urgent, constantly in flux, motivated by random influences, unseen currents, and crises in an ever-shifting sea.

   Spinning a wheel of fortune inside my head, my thoughts rattled around, landing on one thing or another: How could I get rid of the stutter that plagued me? Would my attempt at a *Little Women* haircut even remotely resemble Katharine Hepburn's? (Alas, the answer was no.) How would I lose the fat that encased me? These were some of the random "plans" I pondered, but they led nowhere.

While I was living with Auntie Ger, she never brought up the possibility of my making choices about the direction my life might take; nor did Surrogate Foley who was my legal guardian, ever bring up anything about my future, a long-term look at my life. Although I did dream about what I wanted to be when I grew up, I had no idea that I could make decisions that would determine my future.

It would have reassured me to have a plan, a direction, to move toward, but even as an adult, I have found this elusive. I've achieved some of my goals, but rarely in the way I expected. Without plans, I believe in dreams, even if sometimes they melt like ice cream.

Did anyone ever talk to you about money? Did they prepare you for the money you inherited when you turned twenty-one?

Ah, money, money, money!

It was a shock in February 1945, when I turned twenty-one, and was escorted into the vaults of Bankers Trust by a team of guardians and attorneys congratulating me on the $4.5 million now in my charge. None of it seemed real.

Hard to believe, but no one had ever discussed this inheritance with me. Naney, though obsessed with money, never said anything; nor did Auntie Ger. I hadn't a clue how cautious I should be, or how I should handle it.

I wish I had known then that the greatest gift of money is the independence it can give you. If you are lucky enough to have money, learn how to hold on to it, but don't be a miser, because it will shrivel your insides and start showing on your face in ways that will startle you. "To give is to receive"—and all those other platitudes we come upon now and again—is actually true.

What I did know about money was how to spend it on friends and family, charity, and myself. This is another failing I have to keep close tabs on. But I never doubt that I have the gift of my talents to rely on to make a living. Just when I suspect I am about to fall off the tightrope on which I am balanced, the acrobat pauses, then confidently moves forward. One way or another, a new venture begins and back the money comes!

O y! It makes me nervous to read that. We have such completely different views on this. I just don't believe that one can always rely on one's talents to make money. Talent fades, accidents happen, the world shifts and suddenly a once-prized skill is no longer in demand.

When I was in Sarajevo during the war in Bosnia, I would see people in the market selling whatever possessions they had to earn money. The jobs they once held no longer existed. I bought a broken pocket watch from an elderly man. I didn't need it, but I wanted to help him, and he refused to accept a gift.

In war, societies are turned upside down. If you can fix a motor or wire electricity, you can become a king, but if you have a less practical skill, you will struggle to survive.

When I was a teenager I overheard you on the phone one night telling a friend, "Well, I will always be able to do something to make money."

I froze hearing that. It went against everything I believed, and it still does.

What surprises me about you is that unlike many people who inherit money, you have always had a tremendous drive, a need to create and achieve. I think that is rare. How many children of wealthy or accomplished parents have gone on to make their own mark?

Early on, you and Daddy told me that I would not be inheriting any money and would be on my own financially after college. I'm thankful for that. I never wanted a trust fund, and it has always bothered me when people assumed I had one.

While I was proud of your success, it wasn't mine. I wanted to achieve something on my own.

I am not pretending to be a self-made man. I grew up with

tremendous privileges and advantages that others did not. You paid for my education outright, and I have been lucky in countless other ways. But had I believed there was a financial cushion to fall back on, I probably would have made different choices, and I doubt I would have been as driven. I certainly wouldn't have started working when I was twelve as a child model in order to save up money, calling an agent every day after school to see what auditions or "go sees" there were for me.

Knowing I would have to find my own way financially is another reason I paid more attention to the Cooper side of our family history than I did to the Vanderbilt side. I didn't feel like any good would come of thinking of myself as a Vanderbilt, and I still don't.

Your father was born into a family that didn't have much money, and he wanted you to understand money's value and the importance of hard work. I certainly agreed with his thinking. I'd seen enough of what money could do to families and wanted you to grow up without the feeling of entitlement so many children of wealthy parents seem to inherit.

People who are given trust funds often sit back on their duffs and do nothing. For me, work is the key. The money I have earned through work is the only money I respect. The money I inherited never belonged to me. I felt as though I'd received it under false pretenses. I had not earned it.

M oney is supposed to bring stability to one's life, but your lack of planning has often meant you were surrounded by chaos. I've never understood why you seem comfortable with that chaos. I've worked hard to avoid uncertainty. It is another reason I was so eager to become an adult, so that I could impose order and structure on my life.

I think you would be much happier if you weren't so used to having chaos around you, but I don't think you can allow that kind of stability in your life. It's not something you've ever had.

Chaos does not frighten me. On the contrary, I am comfortable with it. Chaos is my natural habitat. Part of me does long for stability, and always has, but whenever I've achieved it, I haven't been able to let it last. Restlessness is rooted in my nature.

Dorothy Parker wrote, "They sicken of the calm, who knew the storm." And I think that is very true. I was formed by chaos, even before the custody trial, it was always present, although I wasn't able to identify it as such. There was Naney, always agitating, planning, plotting, and whispering; and my mother, moving from one rented house to another, in Paris, Cannes, and London.

Chaos is part of me, like a tattoo.

Tattoos fade, though. They can even be removed.

Yes, but it's very painful to remove a tattoo from one's skin. It takes a long time; you have to go back again and again for sessions.

Am I ever content? Of course, but rarely. Perhaps just momentarily.

Do you know the story by E. B. White, "The Second Tree from the Corner"? On the way from a session with his psychiatrist, a man sees a beautiful small tree with the light hitting it just right. He remembers his doctor asking him, "Do you know what you want?"

Suddenly he knows, telling himself, "I want the second tree from the corner, just as it stands."

Of course, this is something he can never have. It is a fleeting image; it exists only in the moment that he's seen it, and represents the idea of never being satisfied.

I try to create order and stability around me in my home, but it never gets near where the trouble really is, so I always feel the need to change it around again. I decorate a room and I'm enchanted with the changes for a while, but then I think,

"No, no, this isn't right at all; it has to be another way." When I lived at 10 Gracie Square with Leopold, I used to repaint rooms every few months.

Even now, I can't stop changing things around me. I just hung mirrors on one entire wall of my bedroom. I loved the look at first. It had a magical *Alice Through the Looking-Glass* ambience.

"Perfect," I thought.

Now it just seems like a wall of mirrors.

The truth is, and I haven't told you this yet, but I'm considering moving from my apartment. I just heard that the house on Washington Mews in Greenwich Village where Auntie Ger lived is available. Or perhaps I might move into the penthouse apartment at the top of the building I live in now. It has a terrace, and you can see the river. What do you think?

Mom, you are going to be ninety-two soon, and I really don't think moving apartments is a wise idea. You know as well as I do what's going to happen: You'll move into a new apartment and it will satisfy you for a few months, but then the restlessness will return.

Don't worry, I just sneaked that in to shake you up a bit. I know now that moving won't solve the problem, but the impulse is still there.

It's true that I constantly need new stimulation, and I know it is exhausting for everyone around me. Impatience is my biggest weakness. My biggest strength: the ability to harness this weakness.

Well, that last sentence isn't really true. It just sounded good on the page.

I'm still very impatient. I wish it weren't so, but it is. I become enthusiastic, and if something sounds like a great idea, I move on it without considering the long-term ramifications. I plunge forward, without giving it another thought.

I'm working on trying not to do that, but it's hard. I've always relied on instinct, on my impulses. I've been told psychologists consider that a great sign of immaturity, but to me it's a kind of leap of faith.

It's interesting that you recognize your impulsiveness. I don't think you used to. I have always been aware of it, and as you said, it is exhausting for those around you. You get an idea in your head, and then you're suddenly sending out e-mails about it. You don't really think it through. You decide to have a dinner for a few friends at your apartment, and it quickly grows into a party for thirty people whom you then need to entertain at my house because the layout is more convenient. Or you visit a friend in Santa Fe and fall in love with the place and decide you are going to move there, but you haven't really thought through the reality of living in a new city where you know only one other person.

More often than not, I have to be the voice of reason, advising you to slow down or rethink something. It is not very enjoyable being Thomas Cromwell to your Henry VIII. Henry had all the fun, and Cromwell ended up declared a heretic and beheaded, though I do hope to avoid that fate.

Despite our differences, I am just now realizing how much like you I am. It has never really occurred to me before. Though I plan a lot, I do think I am naturally impulsive. It is only by watching you over the years that I have learned to suppress that impulsiveness. I force myself to wait and plan. I run through a range of scenarios and options in my head before I act, and I rarely discuss my ideas with others. I don't want the intrusion of their advice interrupting my thoughts. When I bought the house I live in now, I agonized about it for weeks, silently making financial projections and trying to imagine where I would be in my life and career many years from now.

When Carter was little and couldn't sleep because he was worried about something, Daddy used to say, "Carter, enjoy, enjoy, enjoy."

I don't think that is something you or I do very well. Even

now you're constantly rearranging, redecorating: painting floors, laying down new carpets, moving artwork. It never stops.

Your restlessness was always frustrating to me, but I now see just how impatient I am as well. To others, a room looks fine, but I notice a cable slightly visible behind a speaker, and it becomes all I see. Or I paint a room and it seems all right at first, but after a few weeks want to repaint it. I'm always looking to move on to something new.

I used to have cleaning frenzies as a child. When I felt things were out of control, I would seek to create order over what I could, vacuuming and dusting, rearranging and throwing things away.

Shortly after I told you that your impulsiveness is exhausting, a friend of mine said to me, "It's exhausting being around you." I have to admit that he is right. Even I get tired of the constant churning and planning, the inability to allow myself to simply enjoy, enjoy, enjoy.

With aging you gain perspective, as if looking through a telescope. Your eye focuses and sees things you never noticed before, or never wanted to. I now see so many flaws in myself, things I wish I had done differently.

Looking back on it now, I see how much Sidney loved me, big time. No one in the world did more for me than he did, showering me with love and supporting my career, and yet I was never satisfied.

Toward the end of the relationship, he would say to me, "You're not giving me all of yourself."

Sadly, it was true. After discovering that Leopold was not the person I thought he was, I edited myself in future relationships, always holding something back.

Shortly before he died in 2014, I met with Sidney briefly and was able to tell him how much he meant to me, how much I loved him. It freed me from the tormenting guilt over our split that I'd been agonizing over for years.

When Sidney and I separated, Richard Avedon said to me, "I don't know if the kind of happiness you're looking for exists anywhere."

It startled me then, reminding me of the pain I had caused, the trail of broken hearts that stretched behind me as I'd heedlessly wandered in the forest. It doesn't startle me now. It contains a truth I have only come to understand with time.

Avedon was right: the kind of happiness I was looking for didn't exist. It was what Sontag wrote of, "The inescapable longing for something you never had."

Would it have made a difference if you had understood that at the time? So often, I can comprehend something rationally and intellectually, but it doesn't change the way I feel emotionally, no matter how much I wish it did. Would it have lessened your restlessness, your inability to be satisfied, if you had recognized it for what it was?

I like to think so, but I'm not sure. If you can see your patterns of behavior, and you can understand the motivations behind your actions or emotions, it can help tremendously. It doesn't mean I would not have been restless or dissatisfied, of course, but I might not have acted on those impulses in the way I did.

I've always had passion, what John O'Hara called a "rage to live." Yet part of me craved stability, which is incompatible with that rage.

At the start of my acting career, I read for the part of Carol Cutrere in Tennessee Williams's _Orpheus Descending_. At one point she says, "I want to be seen, heard, felt!"

That's what I wanted, too.

When you feel you have so much to give and so much passion inside you, there is only one thing to do, and that's go out and find it, fulfill it. If you have that rage to live, nothing is going to stop you from trying to satisfy it, and each time you fall in love anew or achieve a creative goal, you tell yourself, "This is it! This is what I've been looking for!" But then you soon start to think, "It's not enough, I want more. I want perfection!"

Your father once said to me, "As time passes, and we grow older, I'm going to love you even more than I do now." That was a new and interesting concept to me, that what we had was enough for him, and would get even better as time went on. It's only a very balanced mind that can think in those terms.

I was thrilled when he said it, but it was alien to me. I'd never thought of the future in that way.

If only I had known then what I now know. I would have sat down and thought about it, seen the rage for what it was. I was born with an appetite for life, a romantic readiness, and I've rushed to greet life with an open heart. I still have it. It is the key to everything. Because of this, no matter how difficult some of my experiences have been, they have not hardened me or made me tough.

If you have that rage to live, don't do something silly and mess up what you already have because you crave more. There is no amount of "more" that will ever satisfy. Once you are aware of this, once you are cognizant of the rage, then perhaps you can see when it leads you astray, taking over your thoughts, propelling you into a course of action you may regret.

When I am unhappy or dissatisfied, I recall what Virgil wrote, "Perhaps some day it will be pleasant to remember even this."

It gives pause, doesn't it?

Whenever you're restless or miserable, if you can imagine that at some point you may look back on that moment fondly, it may make the present more bearable. Even what appears to be a terrible problem may in the future turn out to be a positive change. You just never know.

For all its negative aspects, this restless spirit can, at times, be a blessing. It is the appetite for life that continues to keep one young and alive. It is the key to inspiration that fuels imagination and creativity.

"Never satisfied!" Walter Matthau once described me to his wife, Carol. It was not meant as a compliment. But I take it as one. There is so much to be thankful for, and I am even thankful for my restless spirit.

Four

My father, Wyatt Cooper, was born on a farm in Quitman, Mississippi, in 1927. He attended high school in New Orleans while his mother worked at a factory during World War II, and he eventually enrolled at UCLA, where he majored in theater.

He worked as an actor onstage and on television, and then as a screenwriter. In 1961 he met my mother at a dinner party at the home of a mutual friend. They married in 1963. My brother, Carter, was born two years later, and I arrived two years after that. By then my father was mostly writing magazine articles, one of which led to a book called Families: A Memoir and Celebration, *about his childhood in Mississippi and his belief in the importance of family. He died while undergoing heart bypass surgery in 1978.*

Sidney and I had been together for seven years the evening we went to the actress Leueen MacGrath's house on Sixty-Second Street for a small dinner party. We were the first to arrive and were sitting in her living room talking in front of the fireplace when in walked a tall, knockout-handsome man with the bluest, most piercing eyes I had ever seen or could imagine.

We looked at each other, and that was it. Call it the shock of recognition or whatever you will, but the bond was formed in that instant. And that, Anderson, is how I met Wyatt Cooper.

He had recently co-starred with Uta Hagen in Christopher Fry's *The Lady's Not for Burning*, and was working in Hollywood with Peter Glenville, on a play Wyatt had written called *How Do You Like Your Blue-Eyed Boy Now, Mr. Death?* Lee Strasberg had directed a production of it at the Actors Studio in New York, and Glenville optioned it for the theater.

After that first meeting, I didn't know why or how, only that, hand in hand, we had stumbled into a room and locked the door behind us.

You both came from such different worlds and I like that I am a combination of both of them. The first time I went to a Cooper family reunion it was the summer after I graduated college, the summer after Carter died. He and I hadn't kept in touch with our father's siblings as much as we should have, and once I finished school, I decided to reconnect with them.

The reunion was held at a state park near Quitman, and three of my dad's sisters and one of his brothers attended. I

met dozens of cousins of all ages, and a great aunt as well. It reminded me of a passage my father wrote in his book about the family reunions he attended as a child:

> *To see all those colorful people of such variety gathered in holiday mood, with their jokes and their laughter and their familiarity with each other, was as exciting a thing as I knew. It was better than Christmas. They were my kin. We were of the same blood and bone. I felt related. They belonged to me, and we had claims on one another. We watched each other growing up or growing old, and we felt ourselves to be a part of some timeless process, a process the rules of which applied equally to us all.*

It was the first time I had been with his family as an adult, and the thing that struck me most was seeing that I shared not just a physical resemblance with some of them, but similar gestures and expressions. To discover that the way I laugh or the way I brush my hand through my hair is something hard-wired in my brain, something that other Coopers had done before me and would do long after I was gone, was powerful, and made me feel connected to both the past and the future. It was a feeling I had never had before, and it has stayed with me to this day.

I wish you had been able to feel that with people in your

family: the bonds that exist between generations, links in an invisible chain through space and time.

I, too, wish that I had experienced those kinds of bonds.

Before we married, your father took me to Mississippi to meet his mother and his sisters and brothers. I was overwhelmed. Although he had spoken in detail about his family and what it was like to have parents and siblings, the reality of it came as a shock, and I am not sure I ever got used to it.

Before we married, he said to me, "Lots of happiness ahead for you, little one," and he was right.

We were married in Washington, DC, by a justice of the peace on December 24, and the following day had a party in New York, at 10 Gracie Square, to celebrate. We didn't go on a honeymoon, because we were looking at houses, and when we found the one, on Sixty-Seventh Street, we knew that was where we would live.

Your father had a plan for the life that we were going to have together, but as I told you, until I met him, it had never occurred to me that long-term plans were an option. With him, the pieces of the puzzle started coming together. I was afraid, but eager to reach out and make a grab for what I was seeking.

It happened quickly, our new life: meeting his enormous

family, moving to the new house, your brother Carter born, then you two years after.

I don't think I've ever told you this, but before I was pregnant with Carter, I'd been pregnant with another child but had a miscarriage in my third month. Everything had been moving along so smoothly—no morning sickness, no signs that anything was amiss. I was the happiest woman in the world as Wyatt and I started making plans for life with our baby-to-be.

Oona Chaplin was so thrilled about our news that she sent us a layette of infant clothes, including a yellow wool sweater she had knitted, to welcome our baby. She selected yellow because, at the time, there was no way to test to see if the child was a boy or a girl.

Soon after her gift arrived, it happened. Suddenly, in the middle of the night, I felt contractions as if I were in labor and I found myself hemorrhaging. I was carried on a stretcher down the long stairs of our house and into an ambulance. Nothing could be done, and we lost our baby.

It seemed to take much longer than it actually did to recover, mainly because I agonized that it might be my last chance to have a child with your father. He was by my side throughout the depression I sank into, and his presence made all the difference. Sooner than we could have hoped, I was pregnant again, this time with Carter.

We took joy in the months of expectant happiness and made

no plans for nurseries or layettes until the birth drew near. When Carter was born, we were ecstatic and quickly decided we wanted him to have a sibling.

I was forty-two by then, a difficult age to conceive, so I consulted a doctor, who prescribed a new drug called Pergonal, which was illegal in the United States at the time but available in Italy.

We contacted a friend in Rome, who bought it for me, and I flew to meet him at Charlie and Oona Chaplin's house in Switzerland. Two days later I was on my way back to New York, wearing a muumuu, with Pergonal taped around my waist. I would have been arrested if it had been discovered by Customs, but wild horses couldn't have stopped me.

Nine months later, there you were, Anderson Hays Cooper!

I know you always wanted a daughter, and each time you were pregnant you thought it was going to be a girl. It used to bother me to hear you say that, but I understand why you felt that way. If you'd had a daughter you believe you would have understood her more; it's the same reason that Daddy wanted sons.

One morning several years ago, I woke up and noticed a lump under my eye. When I leaned my head back it disappeared, but whenever I leaned forward, there it was: a small bump under my left eye.

I visited a dermatologist, and he told me it was a fatty deposit and would require a cosmetic procedure to remove. I called you to ask about the surgery, and you couldn't have been more excited. It wasn't that you were happy I had this problem, but you were glad that you had the solution.

"I know just whom to call," you said.

Had I asked for advice on paying my taxes or buying a car, you wouldn't have had any suggestions, but this was something you could guide me on.

"I've made an appointment for you tomorrow. I'll come along," you said when you called back minutes later.

Modern and hushed, the doctor's office felt more like a changing room at a Giorgio Armani boutique.

"Your mother and I have worked together for years," the surgeon said when we were ushered in to see him.

I told him why I had come.

"Well, yes, there is that," he said, his tone indicating that there was other work that might be done. He handed me a mirror and asked me, "What do you see?"

Other than the small bump under my eye, I wasn't sure what I was supposed to be looking at, so I asked him to tell me what he saw. It turned out there were several things I could have adjusted about my forty-something face, and the odd bump I'd come about would require a far more complex procedure than I was ready to undertake.

"I think I'll just live with it," I told you later in the cab as we headed back to your apartment.

"Well, there's no rush," you said. "No don't need to worry about 'fatal beauty' just yet." I sensed a hint of disappointment in your voice. It wasn't that you wanted me to have plastic surgery—at least I hope you didn't—but you seemed disappointed that this opportunity for us to bond had ended.

If you'd had a daughter, you believe there would have been more of these moments. You think you would have known just how to talk to her and be a mother to her. I'm not sure that is really true. I suspect you would still have felt many of the same insecurities.

It is true that I've always believed if I had a daughter we would have bonded from the moment of her birth. I would have guided her to value and respect herself, confiding in her, sorting out with her the details of our lives.

Is this a fantasy? My friends who have daughters say that girls are much more difficult than boys, especially during their middle teen years. I listen, mesmerized, but this idea is so ingrained within me, I am not sure I believe them.

It was through your father's example that I learned what it could be like to be the parent I always yearned to be. Because of him, the concept of planning a life, a family, became real to me.

But it all fell apart when he died. Is loss easier to bear when you know it well? Perhaps. No longer an adversary, it becomes a friend.

I've often thought of loss as a kind of language. Once learned, it's never forgotten. I learned the language of loss when I was ten, and still know it to this day. There have been times when I wished I had a scar or a mark, a visible sign of the pain I still feel over Daddy's death and Carter's. It would be easier, in a way, if people knew without my having to say anything that I am not whole, that part of me died long ago.

Your father once told me that in the small town of Quitman, where he grew up, there were frequent funerals, which the whole town attended. Finally, his mom told him he would have to stop going for a while because it was getting him too upset. That death was such a part of his early life was a revelation to me.

He once said to me, "I don't think we will live to be very old."

I didn't know what he was talking about. When he died at fifty, then I understood. Had I also died then it would have been another person who died, a person your father knew, his wife. Someone very different from the person I am today. If

your father and I met now, would he regard me as a stranger? Would he like me, much less love me?

He had his first heart attack in 1976, then the next year he had another, more serious one. He was placed in intensive care.

When a patient was very ill, the hospital relaxed its rules and allowed children in to visit. We made plans to spend Christmas Day with him and bought a tape recorder to create a memory of our conversation. The presents were wrapped and ready to go, but on Christmas Eve he had another heart attack and was moved into a unit with dying patients.

In the days that followed, I was permitted to be by his side only briefly. Much of the time, he was unaware I was there as he gasped for breath.

One day he seemed to suddenly focus on me and said, "This was not part of my plan."

"But you're *not going to die*!" I shouted back.

He looked startled, as if I knew something he didn't.

"I'm not?" he asked.

"*No*. You're not." And it was true. I believed it.

The next night, January 5, the doctors decided to operate.

I followed as they wheeled him down the hall on a gurney to surgery. He appeared as a man taken from a crucifixion: his body limp, stuck with needles, face unrecognizable, covered with breathing equipment.

I walked by his side, leaning in close, telling him I loved him. He didn't know me.

During the surgery, I waited in a small private room with several friends and your father's sister Marie and her daughter, Beth.

Angel, the nurse on the floor, put her head in the doorway as she departed her shift. "Be brave," she said.

Hours later we heard footsteps coming down the dark, empty, silent hall. It was nearly midnight. "We did the best we could—"

I went home to wake you and Carter. "Daddy's dead," I said.

I remember you sitting on the bed saying that while I looked up at you and Carter. I was sleeping on the floor nearby.

That moment, those two words, reset the clock of our lives. I think back to the person I was at eight or nine, the boy who had a mother, a father, a brother, a nanny he loved; the boy who was funny and not afraid to curl up in his father's lap and show affection and vulnerability.

I think back to that person and know I am a fraction of who I once was, who I was meant to be. As much as I want to break out and laugh the way I once did, feel joy the way I used to, I can't, not fully, not with the abandon that child with a father once knew.

When he died, the thought of him not being in our lives was something I couldn't comprehend. It wasn't just that I was ten years old and didn't understand the finality of death. He loomed so large in all our lives, he so defined our family, that I couldn't imagine us without him.

Many years later I was talking to my former nanny, May McLinden, about Daddy's death. She remembered that the day after the funeral, I said to her, "It will be okay," and she realized I didn't comprehend what had happened.

"Nothing was ever okay again," she said to me softly, all those years later, and I saw that she was crying.

There are times even now when dark thoughts take over. Instead of fighting or pushing them away, I pursue each to its final destination. Entering the tunnel, I know I will circle back, as always, to the place I started from; wishing it had been me who died instead of your father. How much better he would have been at guiding you and Carter, far better than I could ever be.

Carter died at twenty-three. He and his girlfriend had recently separated. When I tried to communicate with him about the breakup, he withdrew, cut me out. If your father had been there, it would not have happened as it did. He understood your every mood and would have had the power to get you both through anything that was happening in your young lives.

When your father and I went together to parent-teacher meetings at your school, I would look around at the other mothers and marvel at how much better equipped they were to be mothers than I could ever be, how much more suited to be wives to my beloved husband.

These were thoughts I never voiced, but they were there, hidden, so painful I tried to block them, focus on being a happy wife and mother, believe that everything was going to turn out all right.

But it didn't.

It was your father who died when it should have been me.

In my deepest heart I know this to be true. I knew this then and I know it now. I have known it since it happened, and I will know it till the day I die: a lifelong sentence with no reprieve.

I hope you know that I do not feel this way.

If things had been different and you died and Daddy lived, there is no telling what would have happened to Carter and me. Who knows the direction our lives would have taken?

What I do know is that I've learned things from you that I never could have from anyone else. You opened my mind early on to the idea that I could achieve anything I wanted if I were willing to work relentlessly for it. It was by watching you that I began to imagine what my own life could become, and I love the life I have now. I am this person because of all that happened, the good as well as the bad. I am this person because you are my mother and you lived and Daddy did not.

Sometimes in high school when I'd visit friends' houses and meet their moms I'd wish you were more like them, more conventional. My friends had kitchens full of home-baked bread and cookies, and their mothers seemed to know everything that was going on in their lives. You didn't cook, and you weren't really aware of what I was doing in school or who my friends were, but the idealization of my friends' moms never lasted very long. The more time I spent at their houses, the more smothered I started to feel.

It was then that I began to see how unique you were. You were never the type of parent to lecture Carter and me or tell us what to do or think.

From the time we were little, you treated us as if our ideas mattered. You and Daddy encouraged us to form our own opinions, and listened when we expressed them. We were not just children in your eyes; we were people who deserved respect. That was a powerful lesson.

It is remarkable how both of you included Carter and me in your lives. I recently found a photograph from the *New York Times* of me shaking Charlie Chaplin's hand when he arrived for a party at our house on Sixty-Seventh Street. He had just returned to the United States for the first time after many years in exile in Switzerland.

We watched his films with you both in the weeks before the party, so that we would understand who he was and what he had accomplished. I was five years old, and I remember when I met him being surprised to discover the youthful little tramp was now a white-haired man of eighty-three.

You even took us to Studio 54. Twice! I am pretty sure that was completely illegal, but it was a fascinating experience, and I've never forgotten it.

I didn't know how rare it was for parents to include their children like that, and it had a tremendous impact on the person I became. It gave me confidence and a deeply held belief that I was valued and worthy.

It was through your father that I learned what a family really was and what it meant to be a parent. Your father grew up talking nonstop about everything with his brothers and sisters and his large family, and he just naturally communicated with you both.

One summer Frank and Barbara Sinatra visited New York and were staying near us with friends, who threw a party for them. Your father and I asked if we could bring you and Carter.

"No way!" Barbara said. "This is a party for grown-ups."

She didn't understand that you both would have been great additions at the party. After all, you were old enough to be seated next to Diana Vreeland and Charlie Chaplin at our dinner table. Needless to say, we stayed home that night.

I am envious of my friends who still have both their parents, but as I mentioned before, I don't believe I would have done all the interesting things I have in my career and my life if I'd known the stability that two parents can bring.

I certainly longed for that sense of safety as a teenager. It would have been nice to have a male figure in those years. It always surprised me that none of the men you were friends with made an effort to reach out to Carter or me after Daddy's death. I kept secretly hoping someone would come forward as a mentor or a friend, occasionally taking me out for a slice of pizza or to a movie.

It is clear to me now just how much I turned inward in the aftermath of Daddy's death, hoping to steel myself against further losses or pain. I started keeping my thoughts to myself, never letting on how much I wished that instead of doing it on my own, I had someone who would guide me.

Did you ever think about getting married again? Many times I wished you would, though I never talked to you about it.

When your father died, I knew I would never remarry. Sidney Lumet did come back into my life. He was getting divorced from Gail Jones, and we started seeing each other constantly—and once again became lovers. He soon asked me to marry him. I seriously considered it, but it was only two months after your father had died, and it was happening too fast.

I wish you had told me that you hoped I would marry again. It would have strongly influenced my way of thinking, my perception of the direction our lives were taking. No doubt, I would have married Sidney. He had loved Stan and Chris and would have extended himself in his devotion to you and Carter.

It really occurs to me only now that there was no man in my family as I grew up, no father or father figure. This is why, after your dad passed away, I didn't think I needed to find a man to be there for you and Carter, but I should have sought a suitable mate capable of loving and supporting us, creating the family your dad would have wanted us to be.

I remember when Sidney came back into your life. I liked him a lot and would have been happy if you had remarried him.

Over the years, Carter and I would meet your more serious suitors, and sing the praises of the ones who seemed stable. Unfortunately, the more reliable and steady they were, the less interested you became.

"He likes sports," you'd say, and we knew you had soured on him.

Or, "He tells jokes," which always meant the relationship was doomed.

Once, when I was older, I remember you described a man you were seeing as "the Nijinsky of cunnilingus." I don't know much about dance, but I'm guessing Nijinsky was pretty limber. I rolled my eyes at you, but you just kind of giggled and looked at me like I had no sense of humor.

"Oh, come on," you said, laughing. "It's funny."

Perhaps the only thing more embarrassing than hearing about your sex life was discovering it was more interesting than my own.

Well, I do think it's important to have a sense of humor about sex and "this funny thing called love," to quote Cole Porter.

Symptoms: weakness in the knees, shortness of breath, pit of the stomach flipping over, heart a whirligig twirling. Looking into someone's eyes, about to faint, while that someone becomes the center of your universe. Is it chemical, or the soul's deepest search to feel complete at last?

Sometimes, unable to sleep, I count lovers instead of sheep. How far back can I go? Unannounced, troubadours emerge from the darkness, parading one after the other before vanishing once again. How fortunate I have been that I have only good things to say about my suitors. Many remained devoted friends, even those who passed like ships in the night and one to whom I bitterly regret behaving badly.

You recently read me a quote by Faulkner: "The past isn't dead, it's not even past." That is true for all of us, but it seems especially so for you. Your past and present seem to coexist. The little girl being led into court by detectives, the teen dreaming in a darkened movie theater, the woman in her twenties in search of a father. You are all those people still, in addition to many others you have been.

So much of our adult lives is influenced by what happened to us as children. It is all still there, the memories, the feelings, and fears, stored just beneath the surface in the hidden crannies of our cortex.

You wanted to right the wrongs of your mother by becoming a mother; Daddy wanted to fix his father's failures as a parent. There are echoes of your mother's passive nature in your own youthful willingness to let strong men determine your actions and choices. Your mother's inability to reach out and talk to you was repeated in your own difficulties early on talking with your kids. There were echoes of your relationship with Dodo in my relationship with May. We repeat patterns without even knowing it or wanting to.

We like to think we are our own people, but sometimes it seems we are just playing out a script that was imprinted in us long ago. I've never asked you what happened to your mother. You said you didn't see or talk with her for fifteen years. How did you reconnect?

After I stopped talking to my mother in 1945, at the urging of Leopold Stokowski, I didn't see her again until 1960.

The therapist's session with LSD that year gave me a new perspective. Perhaps it was also the wisdom and understanding that time brings. But it was confusing. I was ready to forgive, but I wasn't sure who I was forgiving, my mother or myself?

I was still wary of my mother, but I took a huge leap and invited her to tea at my apartment. I have to admit it took all the guts I had to concentrate on the momentous event of once again being face-to-face with her.

My heart was pounding as I opened the door to her, but standing there alone in the hall was a stranger: tentative, beautifully dressed, but hesitant, even fearful. Had we passed on the street, I would not have known who she was or given her a second glance.

Was this my mother?

The person I had feared all my life?

She was suffering from hysterical blindness; no doctor could find anything wrong with her eyes, but her vision came and went. I wondered how she had gotten to my place on her own, but realized someone must have dropped her off downstairs, and the elevator operator brought her into the hallway and rang the doorbell.

Putting my arms around her, I led her into my studio and sat down beside her on the sofa. She asked for a scotch and soda, and I lit her cigarette. I wasn't sure what to talk with her about. The last time I'd seen her I was twenty-one, and by then I was thirty-six. I took her hand in mine, but she pulled it away to pick up her drink.

I wish I could say we opened up to each other, talking of the past and what we hoped our future would be, but we didn't. From the day she walked through that door until the day she died, we never discussed the trial or anything about my childhood. Not once. She wasn't capable of doing so, and I certainly wasn't ready to. I would be now, but back then it was so complicated, and I was still wary of her in many ways.

We kept our conversation polite and on the surface. Despite

your father's support and encouragement of my becoming close to her, because of all the things that had happened and the years of separation, there was no way to begin.

How banal and strange to call all that had happened *things*. As I look at it on the computer screen, the word is little, a meaningless abstract squiggle devoid of the fear, sorrow, and deep regret over the loss and the pain it brought to all of us, Naney, Auntie Ger, Dodo, and to me, changing our lives forever.

After your father met my mother for the first time, he said to me, "She doesn't know one single thing that has ever happened to her." He was right. She was born beautiful, got married at seventeen, gave birth at eighteen, and was widowed a year and a half later. I cringe in pain imaging how stunned she must have been during the custody case, as if hit by a bus.

During the long years of separation, I had tried to forget her, but she never left. She stuck in my gut like glue.

One night in my dressing room, after I'd appeared in a play, thinking about my mother's admiration of the anorexic thinness of the actress Constance Bennett, I asked my friend Russell Hurd, "Did I look thin onstage?

"Yes, darling," he assured me.

"No! No! I mean thin, really, *really* thin?

"*Yes! Really, really, really thin!*"

"That'll show the old bitch," I screamed, to his surprise.

Now here she was, back in my life, sitting by my side. It

drained all my wits and energy to keep a toehold on the tenu-
ous tightrope my unsteady feet were attempting to negotiate.
I found myself fighting an avalanche of hostility toward her,
realizing just how misguided she had been as a parent, how
self-involved and narcissistic.

When I was seventeen and went to visit her, and started
dating completely inappropriate men like Errol Flynn and Pat
DeCicco, she never warned me about what I was doing. What
she wanted was to get me back from Auntie Ger, and she did
that by letting me do anything I wanted, no matter how risky.

Several months after we reunited, in the summer of 1961, I
visited Los Angeles with Stan and Chris, and I went to see her
at the house she still shared with Thelma. I rang the bell, and
Wannsie opened the door.

"Oh, Miss Gloria," she said, welcoming me, "It was all just
a terrible misunderstanding." This was such a mild description
of the tumultuous events we had all been through, I couldn't
help but laugh as I hugged her.

Thelma suggested we rent cottages for a week next to each
other on the beach in Malibu. I was excited because Stan and
Chris would have a chance to spend some time with their
grandmother and great-aunt, not to mention my having time
with my mother, perhaps even to get to know her a little bit
better.

Wyatt joined the family get-together, which was at first

a cautious reunion, but by week's end a huge success. My mother and Thelma usually slept late but joined us for lunch and dinners.

The first day we settled in, Thelma casually mentioned that Harry Richmond also lived somewhere nearby in Malibu.

"Harry Richmond!" I shouted, almost falling off my chair. When I was eleven, Harry Richmond was a hugely popular singer, as well known as Sinatra was years later. I had collected and treasured his records, playing them over and over at Auntie Ger's. He performed at the Club Richmond back then, which was close to New York City, just across the East River. My mother, knowing how much I admired him, had wanted to take me to hear him, but she knew Surrogate Foley, who was my legal guardian, would have had a fit.

"Let's invite him for dinner," Thelma now said, and sure enough that very night, stepping out of an old Chevy, appeared Harry Richmond in full stage makeup, dressed in a top hat and white tie and tails!

There were big hugs all around, but he was clearly eager to start the show. And what a show it was! His voice was no longer what it had once been, so he lip-synced to his old records, which he had brought with him, gesturing as he slowly moved around the room mouthing the words to "The Night Is Young and You're So Beautiful," and other songs I had played in my bedroom in Old Westbury long ago.

It was surreal to be there now with my mother, a family at ease, happy in the moment. An evening never to be forgotten, and not just because I got to meet Harry Richmond at last, but because it brought me close to my mother in a way I had never been before. That week in Malibu, I hadn't been suspicious of her, not for one minute.

Alas, though she came back into my life, we never really connected. It was too late. In all the times we saw each other after reestablishing contact, the conversation rolled politely along without long silences, but we never broke through to each other's heart.

I've never forgotten an intense conversation between my mother and her older sister Consuelo that I'd unexpectedly interrupted once as a child. My mother's back was toward me, but Consuelo saw me as I entered the room, and she grabbed my mother's arm and hissed at her, *"Cuidado, cuidado!"*

The word stuck in my mind. I wrote it down and later looked up the English translation: "Be careful! Be careful!"

I knew then that they had been speaking of things they didn't want me to hear.

Secrets and fear. That is what there had always been between us.

All that is long gone.

How can any of this be of importance or value to you right now? Maybe it will be useful only in the future to assure you that with age everything, yes, everything, in one way or another, falls into place. You can face your past in a way you never thought possible: confidently, securely, and without fear.

I t is so sad that you never discussed the trial or anything about what happened between you. Now of course you would be more than capable of doing so, but it also says a lot about her that she didn't bring up the past, either. It shouldn't have been all on your shoulders.

How did your mother die?

Five years after we reconciled, she and Aunt Thelma were planning to stay in our house on Sixty-Seventh Street, to be there when Carter was born, but before they were to come, she fell ill. It turned out to be cancer and she was dying. Within days she was hospitalized in Los Angeles.

I spoke to my mother on the phone a few hours after giving birth. She had hoped for a girl, as had I. "The third Gloria," I'd promised her. Knowing how ill she was, I nearly lied and told her I'd finally had a girl, but I didn't.

"Another boy!" she said, "Gloria, you're going to start a baseball team."

Those were her last words to me. She died shortly after. She was sixty.

I had to stay in the hospital with Carter, so your father went alone to Los Angeles to attend the funeral. Her death had little reality for me. Who was she, really? Someone I had never known. Someone I had longed for once, a longing that by then felt like it was someone else's.

For decades after she died, I tormented myself with the fantasy that she lived around the corner from me, close, close as could be, and we could speak daily. I imagined visiting her, or her strolling around the block and stopping by for a cup of tea and a cozy chat, eager to hear about my latest adventures and offer her wise counsel.

In this fantasy she remained as lovely as the image I once had of her in Paris: coming in and going out, her long black tresses marcelled into a beguiling chignon, wearing one of her simple black dresses, the huge Marquise diamond engagement ring presented to her by my father still on her left hand beside the gold wedding band.

She'd sit beside me on the sofa, and it no longer bothered me that it was a light scotch and soda she sipped instead of tea; no longer bothered me that she lit one cigarette after another; the smoke became perfumed incense. In this fantasy, nothing about her bothered me. Instead of the passive, exquisite creature hoping to be Her Serene Highness Princess Hohenlohe, she had metamorphosed into a wise, chatty combination of Dr. Ruth Westheimer and Mother Teresa.

But this fairy tale is always replaced by the memory of another trip to Los Angeles after we reconciled. I flew there hoping to see her right away, wanting to talk with her, and perhaps finally open up about all that had passed between us.

I called her from the airport. "Mummy, I'm here," I said, my voice nearly breaking. She could tell I was upset.

"Oh, darling," she said. "I'd love to see you, do please call me when you're feeling better."

It wasn't malicious. She was simply incapable of expressing real emotion and felt no motherly connection to me. I visited her later during that trip, and she pretended as though I had never called upset, and I made no mention of it, either.

There are times when I am overcome with sadness, feeling as if my mother were present with me here in my room. Is it because I am wearing a white wool sweater she knit for me once long ago? After she gave it to me I put it away and didn't take it out until recently, so many years after her death.

Lately I find myself wearing the sweater a lot. The wool is soft, and because it has no buttons, I can easily wrap it around myself for warmth if it is chilly. It works well as a bed jacket, for when I sit up at night reading before I turn out the light. It fits just right, blending into my body, warm and cozy. I imagine her hands once holding the skeins of wool that now encircle my body, touching the needles knitting intricate patterns as she and Aunt Thelma sit in their house in Beverly Hills talking of this and that.

I am sad for her, no matter if she loved me or not. Sad that her life took the path it did and that she knew so little happiness. Sad that as I sit here writing and wearing this sweater, I feel closer to her than I ever did when she was alive. But let's not end on a sad note. Merry Christmas to all and to all a good night.

D o you think you are like your mother at all?

Am I like her? I never knew her well enough to say, but perhaps I may be more like her twin, my aunt Thelma, who was much more outgoing, with an appetite for life and, I suspect, a rage to live. By contrast, my mother was passive, remote, and out of reach.

W hat about Dodo? We haven't talked about what happened to her after the court decided she was not a good influence on you. You said that she attended your wedding to Pat DeCicco. How did you reconnect with her?

I was not permitted to see or speak to her by phone from the time I was ten until I was seventeen. I assuaged the aching grief of the loss by writing to her at the home of friends where she was staying, a Mr. and Mrs. Schiller in Freeport, Long Island. No one ever told me I couldn't write her, and Naney gave me the address.

Dodo changed her name after the publicity brought by the custody trial, so my letters were addressed not to Miss Emma Sullivan Keislich, which was her real name, but to Mrs. Emily Prescott. What matter Emma or Emily? To me, she was my adored Dodo.

This is how we stayed in contact with each other until I was seventeen. Planning to visit my mother for the disastrous trip to Beverly Hills, Auntie Ger said I could go see Dodo. For some reason the court order no longer seemed to apply.

Freddy drove me to the Schillers' tiny home on a long street with houses on each side, every one looking like the one beside it.

And there she was waiting at the door. A line from an old song she used to sing to me popped into my head: "You and I together, love / Never mind the weather, love."

Her arms once again around me, I knew I was home. She led me up to her room, on the second floor of the Schillers' house, where a tray on a bureau held hot chocolate, whipped cream, and cookies studded with sugar that sparkled like diamonds. Sunlight filtered into the room through an oak tree planted in the sidewalk below. Her single bed took up most of the room, but there was space enough for us to sit side by side.

I cried out, "Never leave me again! Never, never, never again leave me!"

Of course it was a silent scream from inside that no one heard but me. I knew from that day on that I would die if I were ever to be parted from her again.

In the years that followed, Dodo became part of every facet of my life. She lived with me in Junction City, Kansas, during the two years Pat DeCicco was at Fort Riley, and during my marriage to Leopold Stokowski, she often spent weeks with me while he was touring. Each month I gave her a hefty amount of money in cash.

Later, when Leopold and I bought the apartment in New York at 10 Gracie Square, Dodo moved into her own suite connected to it. She was there when Stan and Chris were born. As an adult, I found it calming just to be in a room sitting with her.

But nothing lasts forever, and the "never, never again leave me" that I secretly vowed to myself when I was reunited with her was shattered when I fled from Leopold with Stan and Chris and began a new life, with new loves and a growing belief in myself.

I began to see her less and less, and when I met your father, I think he disapproved of her, feeling that she had helped turn me against my mother. We included her in our life only now and then, but Dodo was thrilled with the happiness I had found when I married him. As a wedding gift, she presented me with a dozen crystal goblets in forms of various deities. "Because you are Wyatt's goddess," she lovingly declared as I unwrapped the package.

I wanted to explain to your father what Dodo meant to me, that she was my real mother, but it was so scrambled in my mind, so complicated, that I could never articulate it in a way that would make him understand.

By 1973, she was far from my mind, and I am saddened to admit, I had let her slip from my life.

We were living in the house on Sixty-Seventh Street when a letter came from Catholic Charities. I opened the envelope and read part of the first handwritten line: "I am writing regarding Emily Prescott . . ."

The name jumped out and hit me in the face. Unable to breathe, I tore up the letter without reading any further. I put it in the fireplace and lit a match to it, then ran up the stairs to my bedroom and lay on the bed, silently shaking with dread. I told no one.

I don't understand. She had been closer to you than your own mother, the most important person in your life. Why didn't you read the letter?

This haunts me to this day. Why had months and then years passed by without our seeing each other and rarely being in touch? Perhaps it had something to do with my real mother's re-entry into my life, which was around the time I started distancing myself from Dodo. My mother and I had so many conflicting, unresolved issues that were very difficult to deal with, and I felt the pressure of trying to get pregnant after having had a miscarriage.

All those years later, when I saw the name "Emily Prescott" in the letter, I knew something must be wrong, terribly wrong. I was consumed with confusion and guilt over my betrayal of my beloved Dodo, but I couldn't face it. The only way to deal with it was to behave as a hysterical child would, pretending that this letter, which made my heart pound with terror, simply didn't exist. All it took was a match.

A week later another letter from Catholic Charities arrived. This time it was typewritten, signed by Marjorie Lewisohn, a childhood friend's oldest sister, who was a doctor and had operated on Dodo a few years before, when she needed a mastectomy. Your father and I visited Dodo at Lenox Hill Hospital after the operation, and I brought her a box of her favorite Godiva chocolates. Throughout the visit, your father was polite, but I could tell he was there only because he knew it meant something to me. He clearly disapproved of her.

The letter was brief, informing me that Emily Prescott had died "peacefully in her sleep" at Catholic Charities. There was no mention of the note sent the week before, which I realized must have been from an aide passing on Dodo's dying wish: to see me one last time to say good-bye.

Her death hit hard. I sobbed and sobbed, my grief almost pulling me over the edge.

"All the king's horses and all the king's men / Couldn't put Humpty together again," or so it's said.

But here I am, once more put back together again. That I was not by Dodo's side to see her through to death, as she had been by my side to see me through in life, is one of my greatest sorrows and haunts me to this day.

I now know the cemetery where Dodo is buried under the name Emily Prescott. I plan on visiting her grave soon. Perhaps on the same day I will visit another not-so-distant grave, that of my Naney Morgan. I have never seen either grave, and I wonder what epitaph is etched on each. Will such a visit answer questions I still puzzle over? Do I really want to know the answers? Am I strong enough to?

====

Growing up, I knew about Dodo mostly through my mother's artwork. She would often paint images of herself as a little girl holding Dodo's hand. I think of my mother first and foremost as an artist. She's had numerous solo shows and continues to paint in her studio every day. But to many Americans my mother is best known for the line of designer jeans she launched in 1979. They were the first hugely successful designer jeans and led to her involvement with other clothing lines and fragrances. Though she had little interest in business, she appeared in commercials and print ads and traveled throughout the country promoting her brands.

My brother and I were in our early teens when she started the jeans business, and we used to play a game counting how many women we saw on the street with our mom's name on their rear pockets. It wasn't the first time I realized she was well known, but it was a level of fame I wasn't used to. There are still clothes produced with my mom's name on them, but she no longer has any involvement in the business.

====

A series of unexpected events led me to become a designer. I had my first solo show of paintings in 1948, when I was twenty-four, but in 1967, after a show at the Hammer Galleries in New York, I was invited to appear on Johnny Carson's show with some of my artwork.

Watching Carson that night was Lewis Bloom, president of Bloomcraft, a company that manufactured high-quality decorative fabrics. He thought my artwork would translate well into fabric designs and called me the next day to propose going into business together.

I was the first designer to go on tour, introducing the collection in stores throughout the United States. With the success of the fabrics, I began to design other home furnishing products: sheets, towels, shower curtains, bathroom accessories, kitchenware, plates and glasses, flatware, and so on. I then began designing scarves based on my paintings, and then later, blouses for a company called Murjani. Warren Hirsch, Murjani's CEO, was a merchandising genius, and we came up with the idea of adding designer jeans to the collection. The jeans were released in 1979, and Warren launched a gigantic promotion to support them. I appeared in television and print ads, and it was fun. Although my acting career was behind me, I enjoyed selling the jeans. It was as if I were onstage once again, in a production I'd created and believed in.

The jeans were a success seemingly overnight. Young and old were wearing them everywhere, which surprised everyone, me included. I'd be walking down the street, and women would stop to talk to me about the difference the jeans made in their fashion life. I liked the feeling that I had interpreted a classic item of clothing in a way that gave a woman a positive boost, making her stand tall and be happy about the way she looked, as good fashion always does.

They were a superior product, and I was proud of the success, but it was bittersweet. Your father had died the year before the jeans hit the market, and without him by my side, I often felt very much alone, and I didn't know whom to trust.

An avalanche of money was suddenly pouring in. Warren Hirsch looked me straight in the eye and said, "You're making more money than Commodore Vanderbilt!"

Not quite, but it was nice to see my hard work pay off. I am an artist, though, not a businessperson, and was ill-equipped to manage this money. I found myself surrounded by strangers itching to offer their "help."

I should have kept working with Pearl Bedell, my former business manager, but instead, insecure and shaken, I was influenced by those who wanted Pearl out of the picture, and I fired her. I've always regretted that.

Remember, whenever money is involved it brings out horrific things in people. It has the power not only to split families apart but to destroy the foundation of one's life. Never lose sight of this. Take time and be certain you place your trust in those whose interests and goals mirror your own.

———

To cope with the pressures of business and single motherhood, my mom began seeing a psychiatrist named Christ L. Zois, who recommended his best friend, Thomas A. Andrews, as an attorney to handle all her business dealings.

Zois became my mother's closest confidant. My brother and I became friends with his son, and our families used to vacation together. I thought it odd that a psychiatrist would see one of his patients socially, but I was young and didn't give it too much thought.

In the late 1980s, my mother discovered that she was being defrauded by Andrews and Zois. Not only had they acquired some of the rights to her name, but Andrews had not paid her taxes for years. It was a betrayal that left her reeling emotionally and in debt to the IRS. Eventually Zois lost his medical license in New York State, and Andrews was disbarred.

How could this happen? It happened because I trusted them completely. I even recommended Zois to Oona Chaplin, whom he was also accused of swindling.

Had I been a suspicious person, I would likely have seen the warning signs in Zois's relationship with Andrews, but if you can't trust your doctor and your lawyer, whom can you trust? I lost millions and part of my business, and spent years paying back taxes, but I believe that what goes around comes around. Andrews is dead, and Zois has been disgraced. Still, I never recovered the money the court ordered them to pay me.

I wrote to you before about never wanting to become hard, about always wanting to be open and trusting. The downside of being open is that you can easily be hurt, and I have been many times. The betrayal by two people I trusted completely was a hard blow to recover from. It exploded the core of my being, and made me wary of ever trusting a psychiatrist or attorney again.

I believe in forgiveness, because without it, your spirit is not free, but this betrayal took time, courage, and a lot of faith to overcome. I have swept these two men from my mind and into a garbage heap in the Great Beyond, where they will be very much at home.

There were times when I was facing financial ruin that I

considered marrying for security, but it was not something I could actually bring myself to do. Zois and Andrews robbed me of financial independence, but they did not take my emotional freedom.

Had I married a man for security, without loving him, would it have made me happy? Would I have been capable of making him happy? I think not.

At my lowest ebb, an angel descended: Bill Blass, an acquaintance I hardly knew, came forth with incredible generosity, keeping me financially solvent for years until I was able to do so once again, on my own.

When my friend Nancy Biddle wrote to thank him, he replied, "Well, somebody has to."

It astonishes me still that he would do this for me, a person he hardly knew.

What did not astonish me was the actual betrayal by Zois and Andrews. I was hurt by it, deeply, but I fought back immediately. I was trained in childhood by masters to roll with the punches. If I were walking on the street and someone threw acid in my face, it would not faze me. I don't think I would miss a step.

I was devastated by the greed of those I trusted, but I should not have been. I learned of greed early through Naney, who watched over her stock portfolio as tenderly as she hovered over me. For the last few decades of her life, she lived more than modestly in one tiny hotel room, a bottle of milk kept cool on the windowsill, her meager wardrobe worn for years. All the while, on the pages of her stock portfolio, a considerable fortune accumulated. Many times I tried to get her to move to a nice apartment that I was happy to pay for, but she always refused.

I adored her but could not grasp her values, her tight fist clinging to things I didn't understand. No matter how much I tried to shower her with beauty and luxury, it meant nothing to her.

Do I have greed? Yes, but not for money, even when I didn't have it. My greed is for beauty.

I think I would have gotten along with Naney Morgan very well. She was practical and knew exactly what was important to her and what wasn't. The gossiping about society people would have annoyed me because I don't care about that kind of thing, but I love the fact that she lived simply in one room even though she had a big stock portfolio. That doesn't sound like greed; that sounds like heaven!

No chaos, no stress, no high overhead, just money in the bank to fall back on if times get tough. That was actually a dream of mine when I was a child, to live very simply but have money in the bank that could be used in emergencies to help those I cared about and people in need. I wish I had her discipline!

Yes, Andy, come to think of it, you and Naney would have been a match made in heaven!

Five

In 1988, my twenty-three-year-old brother, Carter, killed himself. It is still hard for my mom and me to understand what happened. There is not a day that goes by that we do not think about his life and his death.

Carter graduated from Princeton University in 1987 with a degree in history and was working at American Heritage magazine when he died.

A few months before he killed himself, he came to my mom's apartment disheveled and upset. He talked about quitting his job and moving back home, though he had his own apartment in the city. I was in New York that weekend, and when I saw him, I got worried. He had recently broken up with his girlfriend and seemed to have lost his usual confidence. He appeared scared, as if his thoughts were racing.

The following week, I returned to college in Connecticut, and Carter started seeing a therapist. He seemed to snap out of whatever funk he'd been in, and I was so relieved, I didn't ask him again about what had happened.

We talked occasionally on the phone, but I didn't see him again until the weekend of July 4. We ran into each *other by chance on the street in New York and went for a quick lunch together.*

"The last time I saw you, I was like an animal," he said. I was happy he could make a joke about it, and didn't question him further. Perhaps he wanted me to, but I didn't. I wish I had.

It was the last time I saw him alive.

On July 22 he came to my mom's apartment once again. He appeared distracted, not to the degree he had been in April, but enough to concern my mom, who spent much of the day with him. In the late afternoon he took a nap, and at around 7:00 p.m. he woke up and walked into her bedroom.

"What's going on?" he said, seemingly disoriented.

"Nothing's going on," my mom assured him.

He ran from her room and up the stairs of the duplex apartment, through my room, and out onto the balcony. When my mom caught up to him, he was sitting on the ledge fourteen stories above the street. She tried to talk to him, begging him to come inside, but he refused. A plane passed overhead, and after looking up at it, he spun off the ledge and hung from the side of the building, his hands holding on to the balcony.

After a few seconds, he let go.

ANDERSON COOPER and
Gloria Vanderbilt

I have heard it said that the greatest loss a human being can experience is the loss of a child. This is true. The person you were before, you will never be again; it doesn't just change you, it demolishes you. The rest of your life is spent on another level, the level of those who have lost a child. If you are blessed with other children, you go on living to be there for them, but the loss will consume you at unexpected times for the rest of your life.

Just yesterday a moment clear as the day it happened flashed into my mind.

Carter, age six, at our house in Southampton, jumps out of the pool, exuberantly running toward me to hug me. "Mommy, I want to marry you!" he yells.

Hundreds of treasured moments: your father holding Carter as a baby, dancing around the room on a night when he couldn't sleep, singing along to a Jobim bossa nova playing softly in the background. Carter, as a teenager, coming into my dressing room for the first time at 10 Gracie Square after we had just moved in, while, outside, fat flakes of snow swirled.

"Oh, Mom," he said, "It's such a hopeful room."

And it was.

I will remember everything about him forever.

Is the pain less? No, just different. It is not something you "work through"; it is not something that goes away or fades into the landscape. It is there forever and ever, inescapable until the day you die.

I have learned to live with it. Carter died twenty-seven years ago. There are times he comes to me in dreams, appearing as he would at the age he should be now. But these are fleeting images that vanish as I try to hold on to them. Carter is not here. He has no brilliant career. No loving wife he is crazy about. No son named Wyatt. No daughter named Gloria. He . . . they exist only in memory and on this page.

I love to talk about him to his friends. Recently someone whom I hadn't seen in a while and who knew Carter told me she thought it might be too painful for me to speak of him, and was somewhat surprised when I told her how happy it made me to do just that. It brings him to me. He is not forgotten. How proud today he would be of you and what you are making of your life.

I imagine you two interacting, not as you did as children, but today, as men. Your father is there, too. But these images fade quickly as well.

Only you and I are left. Even though I don't get to see you as much as I'd like, because you are so busy, I do get to see you every night on a TV screen, and what better gift could a mother receive?

So thank you, God or Whoever or Whatever is in charge of things. I have no complaints.

You and I are different in how we handle grief. I know for you it's important to talk to people. I remember in the days after Carter's death you would tell everyone who came to the apartment what had happened. Reliving the horror over and over again helped you and I was glad something did, but I found it hard to talk about what I was feeling. In times of crisis, I grow silent. I wish I were better at talking about painful things.

After Carter's death, I sensed your withdrawal, which continued on into the weeks that followed, as friends came to the apartment hoping to bring solace to our grief.

I lay in bed in my room unable to stop crying, a verbal stream of details pouring out, going over it, again and again, talking about how it happened. If indeed you did actually spend long stretches alone with me, I don't remember them.

But I knew you were in the apartment somewhere, talking with others, especially Carol Matthau, my lifelong friend, who had arrived from California. I knew this because she told me that the two of you had long conversations alone, although she kept their contents secret from me.

Although at first I was aware of your distance from me, and upset by it, soon the waterfall of tears that kept flowing from me washed away any awareness that you were shutting me out.

I wanted to die and I knew that only the stream of pain I kept going over and over and over again was what was keeping me alive.

A month after Carter died, you had to go back to school. You didn't want to go, but I knew you should. The day you left, you gave me a letter.

"From now on we are partners," you'd written. I felt that, too.

But soon after, you said to me, "Don't drink."

It stunned me that we were not as close as I had thought, that you were unaware that even though I was once again besieged by grief, I would never have turned to drinking to dissolve my pain.

I did feel we were partners and still do, now more than ever. What I said about drinking was that I couldn't be as close to you as I wanted in the wake of Carter's death if you began to drink again. I didn't think you would turn to alcohol immediately, but I feared you eventually would. If you had, it would have been impossible for me to remain close to you. I would have shut myself off from you for my own protection.

After Daddy died, you didn't drink for several weeks, and I thought perhaps you never would again, but then one cold winter's day I came home from school and I could tell that you were drunk. Alcohol transformed you into another person and left me angry and feeling very alone.

You didn't drink after Carter's death, however, and I am so proud of you for giving up alcohol altogether.

It is strange for me to talk about this with you. For my entire childhood, this was something that was never spoken about in our house. Your drinking, occasional and unpredictable as it was, felt like a constant presence, and yet it was never discussed. How many silent dinners did I sit through pretending I didn't notice?

You mentioned drinking as a teenager that summer in Los Angeles, when you lived with your mother, and you alluded to her drinking as well. Was that when it began for you?

Though I'd started drinking sherry before going out on dates that summer of 1941 in Los Angeles, it was not until my marriage to Leopold that a pattern emerged. It was infrequent at first, but toward the end of our marriage I began to have spells of drinking and sobbing. The first time it happened, Leopold was by my side, and he put his arms around me, saying, "Pray to Divine Mother," the deity he believed in.

I hadn't a clue what he was talking about. I kept sobbing and couldn't stop.

I lived in terror that I had inherited the alcoholism of my father. My beautiful, generous half-sister Cathleen, my father's daughter from his first marriage, was also an alcoholic. I never even knew of her existence until I was fifteen and Auntie Ger told me I was to meet her. She had waited to introduce us, to make certain Cathleen would not drink in my company. She never did.

Episodes of drinking and sobbing came and went as thunderclaps erupting in dark night. I would pass out into sleep and awake the next morning with a headache, but no memory of why I had been crying. The waves of tears had washed me back on the shore, safe and sound, but once again balanced on the tightrope.

These episodes were never a daily occurrence. A look in the mirror at what drink and tears did to my face shocked me. (Vanity! Vanity!) I was too preoccupied with beauty to risk continuing. Purged and clear, I'd press on. But time would pass, and the pattern would repeat itself.

I needed someone to talk to, but betrayed and lied to by

Leopold, I found he was no longer the god I'd worshiped, trusted, and adored.

The fear I might lose control led me to the psychiatrist I mentioned, Dr. McKinney. Well into my time in therapy, I asked him if he thought I was an alcoholic like my father and my half-sister.

"No," he said, "you like being independent too much."

D o you think Mom is an alcoholic?" Carter once asked me when we were in high school.

I was so shocked he said that word out loud that I didn't know how to respond. We had never spoken of it before. Each of us dealt with it in silence. I was so surprised to hear him use the word that I dismissed his question, and never spoke with him about it again. Put off by my silence, he never attempted to, either.

Your drinking made it difficult to trust you. I never knew what I would find when I came home from school each day. I dreaded going anywhere with you, worried that you might start drinking: on planes, at restaurants, parties. The person you became scared and angered me. I was never sure if you were aware of what you were doing. I assumed you were, but I didn't know.

The day after you'd drunk too much, it would be as if

nothing had happened. It added another element of danger and fear to our lives, and contributed to the feeling that we were somehow adrift. Even now, typing this out, I feel that fear. I can remember it and realize I have spent much of my adult life making sure I never feel that way again.

It means the world to me that you have come to trust me enough to express the feelings you have accumulated over the years about my drinking episodes. I can only imagine the courage this took. It is more than brave, considering the close relationship we now share.

It has been twenty-seven years since Carter's death, and despite all the difficulties I have faced since then, I no longer have an issue with alcohol. At ninety-one, my liver and heart are healthy, as they have been throughout my life, and instead of an alcoholic, I am a workaholic.

As for the years before, I am sorry for the times I disappointed you as a mother. My flaws are rooted in things that happened way back in the beginning, as they are for most people, and I hope that knowing me now as you do, you understand where they came from, and can find it in your heart to forgive me.

You have proved, by your life and what you have made of yourself, that you have triumphed over whatever shortcomings I may have had as a mother.

Recently you asked me, "Do you think you are like your mother?"

I told you that I never really knew her, so how could I answer?

Well, the answer is, perhaps I am.

I don't view these things as failings, and I certainly understand their roots, more now than ever. As I said, I am very proud of you. I certainly don't think you are like your mother now. Perhaps you once were. How could you not be, even though she wasn't involved in your life? But you forged your own path, and broke the cycle that was set in motion long before you were born.

You have done so much with your life, touched so many people. You are open and honest, and you can reach out to others in ways your mother never could.

We have never spoken of forgiveness, and I have no knowledge what your thoughts, or doubts, if any, are on the subject, but I still smile thinking of the line from the Lord's Prayer, which Dodo taught me and which I'd repeat every night kneeling by my bed before jumping in to sleep, "Forgive us our trespasses as we forgive those who trespass against us."

I hadn't a clue what it meant, but today I understand, and although it has preoccupied most of my life, I've at last come to know that forgiveness is much simpler than I could ever have imagined: whatever problem you have with someone, project yourself into the other person and see it from their point of view.

When you do this, good and evil shuffle into patterns and you are capable of forgiving trespasses. When you understand from whence the good or evil came, and the other person's actions or motivations, only then can you forgive and let it go. Most children believe that trauma, death, or divorce happen because of something they have done, though they don't understand exactly what; they think it is their fault. I certainly believed I was to blame for all that happened when I was a child. I felt guilty about the custody battle between my mother and Auntie Ger, even though I couldn't understand why. I also thought it was somehow my fault my mother was branded a lesbian.

It was difficult to let go of that. It took me years to understand and forgive her for the pain she caused and to forgive myself for the crippling guilt that has been with me all my life—guilt that has hung over me from the time I found out my father died an alcoholic at forty-five, and my half-sister Cathleen at forty of the same disease.

Finally I figured it out. It was not my fault. I wish it had been different, but I did what I could, as we all do with situations that are handed to us.

At best, I no longer agonize intensely as I did over my failings or the failings of others. I accept them. At worst, I have to admit that somewhere within still lurks a demon of rage. Age makes it impossible to put right the things that went wrong. There is little time left.

I've never heard you mention the demon of rage before. It surprises me, because I have often felt that I, too, am fueled by rage, and I have only ever told a few people that.

It is not the "rage to live" you wrote about before, but rage at the unfairness of losing my dad and Carter. It is like a hot furnace that fuels a ship across the sea, but this rage requires no tending; no one needs to stoke its coals. It burns continuously, powering me forward through calm seas and rough.

Yes, it is different from the "rage to live," but perhaps connected in some way. For me it is rage over much of what happened. Rage at my mother for instigating the custody case against Auntie Ger. Rage at the position I was put in as a child. Had she not done that, and let me stay with my aunt, so much would have been different. I became a pawn in a battle that never should have taken place.

I have no respect for those who harbor self-pity and I have none of it in reference to myself, but the rage is there, burning hot, deep in my core.

I understand now how little I knew you when my father died. I always thought that you and I didn't have much in common and that I was just like him. The fact that he and I looked so much alike made it easier to believe we were so similar.

"Buddy, that boy is the spittin' image of you," his sisters used to say when he would take Carter and me to Mississippi. I'm sure it was irritating for you to hear that, as if you didn't have much of a role in the matter.

I see now just how much like you I really am, how similar we are and always have been. It makes me feel so much closer to you.

I may look like my dad, but I am most definitely your son. We share the same drive and determination, the same restlessness and rage. It is good to know you've felt these things, too, and to see how they have both helped and hindered you.

To quote Elizabeth Barrett Browning: "I love you in ways that are infinite and as in eternity have no beginning or end."

But are we alike?

Sometimes I think hardly at all. You are the living image of your father, not only in appearance, but in valuing the same standards he held in high regard, standards that are sometimes hard to live by.

Other times, yes, we are indeed completely alike. We share sensitivity, tempered by poise and the reserve to reveal only what we wish to communicate.

We have the gift of editing, presenting ourselves in different ways to different people. We are not gossips. We are worthy to be trusted with secrets of family and friends. We have fun going to the movies together, sharing a bag of popcorn. We do not burden each other with trivial troubles, or pull each other down with unsupportive comments. We advise each other on pressing matters from time to time, and you always give me a short, sensible, well-thought-out solution to any problem. I try to respond in the same manner.

We both spend a lot of time organizing our lives, secretly working out various options and scenarios in our heads. Luckily, yours are far more practical, and more likely to become reality than mine, which continue to be influenced by the enchanted fairy tales I read as a child. In spite of this, I treasure those fairy tales still, for they are, in large part, what spur my creativity.

We share a restless spirit; in fact, we are never at rest, and rarely, if ever, will anything satisfy Andy and his mom. Soon something beckons. It's there, around the corner, just out of sight. All we need do is follow.

All my life I have craved and longed for love, and I have not been deprived; my cup hath runneth over, but it was never enough. It never got anywhere near where the trouble really was: no mother and father, as my secret sister Susan Sontag knew about so well.

Here, Andy, thankfully, we are not alike. Even though you lost your father when you were ten, you knew that there wasn't a moment from birth when you didn't have and know his support. How fully, completely, he loved you and Carter. Although only those years were given, they were enough for him to pass on to you the values that have made you the person you are: my son, treasured each moment of my life.

Years ago I asked how you made it through all the traumas in your life.

"I had an image of myself: that at my core there was a rock-hard diamond that nothing could get at, nothing could crack," you said.

It was not a boast. It was a statement of fact. The words were tinged with sadness.

Do you still feel you have that rock-hard diamond in your core, or has that changed with time?

As death approaches, I no longer imagine a diamond at my secret core. Instead, I see shimmering flashes of moonlight on the calm of a midnight sea.

A voice calls across the water, "Forgive me." It is my voice, but I am not speaking to "Our Father, who art in heaven." I'm calling out to those I have hurt. They know who they are. I pray they forgive me, as I forgive those who have trespassed against me.

"Bless me, Father, for I have sinned," the words I banished so long ago, now come foremost to my mind. For me, this has nothing to do with the confessional, but with an acknowledgment of the mistakes I have made. You may find, as I have, that the longer you live, time becomes a giant jigsaw puzzle, with the missing pieces not only unexpectedly discovered, but sliding into place, irrevocably and finally, as *B* comes after *A* in the alphabet. Even if it's too late, alas, to rectify every mistake, what matter the bitterness or regrets? I have found solace in living long enough to understand and forgive the person I once was.

I couldn't have written that thirty years ago. That is one of the things I like about being older. It frees you in many ways. With time, I have come to understand why things happened the way they did, and that has allowed me to forgive myself.

But it is painful, because when you reach this point in life, you know the years left are numbered and there isn't any going back. There is nothing I can do to change what's already happened.

The Moving Finger writes; and, having writ,
Moves on; nor all thy Piety nor Wit
Shall lure it back to cancel half a Line,
Nor all thy Tears wash out a Word of it.

Omar Khayyam wrote that, and he was so right. That is what is difficult about getting old: that finger has already written; you are stuck with it. It doesn't stop me from trying, however. One of the most unexpected things that is happening as

I age is discovering that relationships with those I have loved and lost have changed. It is somewhat like rewriting a story.

The mother I feared has in memory become the exquisitely beautiful woman whom I longed to get attention from as a child. Today I am fulfilled as I pass by her portrait hanging in my living room; she is here now, though she wasn't there then. That is good enough for me.

Dodo, whom I truly loved and who was always there for me, is now, alas, not. It ended tragically, and there remains a scream of silent pain, but she is here in photographs and letters written to me over the years. It must suffice.

And last but not least, Naney Napoléon, mastermind behind the scenes of the whole, terrible mess that affected the lives of those she truly did love. Her "rage to live" was a passion for money and society, not something I admire, but no matter. I love her as I did then, and always will. I say to her now, as she often would say back then, "You are my own flesh and blood."

Six

Sometimes as a child I would see a shadow of sadness pass behind your eyes, and there are moments I see it still. After all we have talked about this year, I have a much better idea where that shadow comes from.

Did you know that after you speak, you often silently repeat the words you have just said out loud?

I used to wonder why you did this, but now I understand. You are reviewing what you have just said, replaying it in your mind. It is a sign of how lost in thought you often are, even in the midst of conversation with other people.

We are very similar in this way, but I am usually lost in thought thinking about the future, and you are reviewing moments from your past. I wish sometimes we could break out of ourselves and just be in the present, but it's not easy for either of us.

Since we've started communicating like this, I hope we will be able to do that, but you are right, I tend to replay moments from my past, imagining how they might have been. Some experiences are more real for me when I play them over in my mind's eye than when they first occurred. Of course, it would be better to be in the scene originally, to "be present," as you say.

This replaying of scenes from my past is one of the side effects of aging. It occurs rarely in younger years when time is speeding by, something new happening every minute. Now when I remember a painful scene from the past, I reconstruct it from another point of view, to make it bearable. I re-edit it, changing the outcome so the story has a happy ending, but sometimes I become overwhelmed and just have to stop.

Do you do reconstruct scenes from your past?

I think about events that have happened—it's impossible not to—but more often than not, I am imagining scenes from the future, unknowable as that future may be. I am always planning, preparing myself for what comes next, and what may come after that, and after that. I find looking backward too painful; there is no reinventing the past for me.

I have drawers full of photographs, snapshots from my childhood, and I keep telling myself that someday I will go through them, but I haven't yet. It's as if I'm compiling evidence, as a reporter gathers facts for a story, but for now I find it too difficult to open the drawers.

Well, I wish I'd had the foresight to consider the future as you do. The idea that I would ever be ninety-one never had any reality for me. It was inconceivable. If it had ever entered my mind, I naively wouldn't have thought it would be all that different. Wow, what a surprise. It certainly is different. No more swinging on the trapeze, no more running up and down stairs, lots more contemplation.

Once upon a time, long ago, women made up charming fantasies about themselves and fibbed about their ages. Until the day she died, Naney skillfully sidestepped the reality that she was eighty-six years old. It was a harmless preoccupation to hold time at bay.

There is something touching about the idea, the trusting hope that it is indeed in our power to control what is happening to our faces, our bodies. Today we can delay the decline, but the inevitable lies ahead. Inside, however, in our core, past the aches, pains and creaking joints of age, youth still resides. Keep that in mind.

As I write this, I am stretched out on a sofa. Flakes of snow drift past the arched windows of my living room. As I look back at my life, I become once again an acrobat on a tightrope, poised, suspended. I close my eyes and take a deep breath. But as I breathe out, I am no longer an acrobat. My life no longer depends on balance. I am free. I am nearly ninety-two, but at this moment I feel ageless.

D o you think about death a lot? Over the years, you have talked to me about dying many times. Plenty of people say they don't want to be a burden, or may discuss a living will or a "do not resuscitate" order with their children, but you have always been a bit more, shall we say, detailed?

You have talked about ending your life on your own terms— taking pills if you were no longer able to enjoy your days.

This used to make me nervous, but the more death I have seen over the years, the more I know that no one can predict how he or she will react as it approaches. In the abstract, people talk about how they want their lives to end, but as the time nears, and the reality becomes clearer, their perspective changes.

This morning I woke up thinking I could have died in my sleep. Instead, here I am ready to go, "Up and at 'em." Over my first cup of coffee it came to me that life starts out as a straight line moving upward, but as we age, it starts curving down ever so slightly, then faster and faster as the years pass, merging into a full circle at death, completing the journey from where we began. No matter how we plan ahead, there is no certainty when the curve will complete itself. It can, might, will at any instant. (Yes, even before I finish my coffee or this next sentence I could die.) No matter what our age, death is not in the distant future. It is here in this present moment, right now, alive and waiting. Accepting this fact puts a different light on how I think about death, and I wish I had become aware of this sooner.

Despite Botox and so on, time is not reversible. It has been marching steadily on since the moment we are born.

"Tramp, tramp, tramp, the boys are marching!"

No secret the destination.

Woody Allen wrote, "Rather than live on in the hearts and minds of my fellow man, I'd prefer to live on in my apartment."

Well, here I am, living on in my apartment. I am not afraid, only apprehensive sometimes that death may happen sooner than I think. I'm not ready yet.

If not in my sleep, I am determined to go into death serenely, not kicking and screaming, but using whatever foolproof medication is available to get the job done. Will I have courage to do this? This is only a possible option in later years, if I'm seriously ill and ready to go.

There have been times when, filled with despair, I thought of taking my own life, but I never wanted to leave you and your brothers with the burden of wondering why.

These thoughts pass. New projects appear unexpectedly, new adventures pull me back into life. My imagination takes charge, giving me strength to edit and reconstruct whatever the current situation happens to be; or I turn a corner and see something beautiful or someone extraordinary running toward me, arms outstretched, ready to fold me in an embrace.

I hope to be around for a while, but I do want to mention some thoughts regarding my funeral. I don't want you scrounging around thinking, "What is she going to wear?" This way you don't have to worry about anything; it's all mapped out for you.

I want to be cremated, and I'd like you to place a handful of my ashes in your father's grave. When I visited Ned Rorem in Nantucket, I noticed a glass jar with an adhesive label on his desk containing what appeared to be small white pebbles.

"What is that?" I asked.

"The ashes of my mother and father," he responded. This was the first time this possibility occurred to me. I had always thought ashes would be dirty, black, like soot in a fireplace after the wood burns down. But it turns out ashes don't have to look like that. I wish I'd known this before, so we could have done this with Carter and your father and have kept their ashes close by.

I told this to Nancy Biddle, and when her son died she kept some of his ashes and found comfort in doing so. If it interests you, please keep some of mine in a jar somewhere. If not, no problem. Just scatter what remains in the ocean on a sunny day.

I had thought not to have a religious service, but maybe something more is required? It's up to you, and however it's easiest. My wishes are whatever you decide.

If you do want to have a funeral in a church, St. James is probably appropriate, as that's where Carter was confirmed and where his funeral took place. If there is an open casket at Frank E. Campbell's funeral home, dress me in one of the Fortuny dresses (the yellow one perhaps), which are in a box in the cedar closet in my apartment. Please have Aki do my hair ("Vanity, vanity, all is vanity"). Also ask him to select someone to do my makeup—I do not want the funeral home's cosmeticians to do it. If Aki and his makeup person are not available, please ask my dear friend Nydia Caro to supervise. She will know exactly what to do.

At the service, I would like to have a number of my friends speak, and please ask my friend Judy Collins to sing "Amazing Grace."

W ell, I think you will be around for a lot longer, but I will be sure to do just as you wish.

You've talked a little about forgiveness and failures. Do you have many regrets?

Ah yes, let us come to regrets and as we do let me sing to you, Anderson, a song I once heard Naney singing as I burst into the room without knocking. She stood as if in a trance, her back to me, looking out at the rain lashing against Auntie Ger's guest bedroom window.

On the wedding finger of her left hand, a gift from her husband, three round diamonds representing her three daughters: Gloria, Thelma, and Consuelo. Her red mahogany nails tapped the windowsill in time as she sang.

Time is flying,
Love is dying,
Youth cannot be bought . . .

She pressed her cheek hard against the glass as if to break it so rain would splash on her face. Then she hummed another melody before once again singing,

Dream, Dream and forget,
Pain. Fear. Useless regret,
Fly, Fly, beautiful lady, on light bright wings.

It made me so sad I wanted to cry, but instead ran and put my arms around her. Where had my adored, and adoring, valiant Naney Napoléon gone?

"Come, little one," she said, "There, there now, don't let's be gloomy. Everything is going to turn out all right!"

And I believed her.

I wish I could be like Edith Piaf, belting out that I have no regrets, but I'm convinced that even the Songbird of Paris had some; why else would she so insistently sing a song denying she had any? My greatest regret is not making more of an effort to be closer to Carter, not talking with him about feelings or experiences we may have shared. Perhaps it would have made a difference in what happened to him. I always imagined we would be closer as adults, once we had lives of our own. I thought there was plenty of time.

For me the list of regrets is so long I wouldn't know where to begin or to end.

It is only today, with the passage of years, that I can look back on choices I made and see how many were mistakes. At the time they seemed like wise decisions, triumphs even.

But the heart of the matter, the nitty-gritty truth, is that I am grateful I was able to pass this way. I wouldn't want to go through it all again, but I am thankful that I was bestowed at birth, by my Fairy Godmother, with the gift of being able not only to give love, but to receive it in return. For I have come to believe that love is all that matters, and I have had more than my share.

So thank you, God, Moosha Moo—remember, from William James's "Anesthetic Revelation"?—or whoever or whatever you might be.

Coming right down to it, I wouldn't have wanted to miss a moment. Well, maybe one or two. And if you flirt with the idea of reincarnation, who knows, we may meet again. But this time, Andy, I promise I will get it *right*.

Earlier I sent you a letter I had written to my long-lost father. I thought I would write one to myself at seventeen, a letter I wish had arrived before I headed to Los Angeles for the "two-week" visit to my mother that changed my life forever.

Gloria,

For you, underneath happiness lies in wait a dragon. If it is mercifully asleep, you are unaware the dragon exists, but it is there, as it has been since those dark nights in Paris when you lay in bed straining to hear the whispers of Naney and Dodo filtering through the half-opened bathroom door.

But now?

I am happy to tell you, I have become captain of mind, spirit, and soul on a boat capable of slicing through seas, rough or calm. Still, the dragon is patient. Though out of sight, it glides along in the pitch-black depths, keeping track of my progress as I chart my course. When I started writing to Anderson, telling him the Tale about all that happened, I felt the dragon quicken its pace. You are unaware, but I now know that my life has been a long search to slay this beast.

But not to worry; let's not be hard on ourselves. I've made the dragon a friend and so can you; the kind of friend who lives in a distant land you touch base with now and again, and only to remind yourself of how far you have come from where you began.

There are a few other things I'd like to get off my chest, as the saying goes, before I pop off elsewhere. Not that it will change anything, just perhaps it will make me feel better about—ah yes—those useless regrets Naney sang about.

So listen, Gloria, while I tell you what might have been had I read this letter before it was too late.

First, I urge you to find a mentor—ideally, a woman in whom you can confide—as soon as you can. You need someone with a lot of life experience, who is open and interested in listening to you, someone with whom you can talk about the tumults raging inside you. You have no one, and have acted impulsively too many times to count.

I remember, particularly in my younger years, there were many times I wished I had never been born. But soldier on, I promise those moments will pass.

Go to college, and afterward, study art in Paris. Don't get married at seventeen; wait until you are older and ready to start a family. You'll know who you are by then. Right now you haven't a clue, though you think you do.

ANDERSON COOPER and
Gloria Vanderbilt

As for marriage, I should be an expert, but I certainly don't feel like one. I suppose I do have a few words of advice.

Do not get married until you are absolutely crazy certain this is someone you can imagine being with for the long haul. Spend a lot of time with him. Travel with him. Traveling together is the best way to get to know a person.

Also, fall in love with someone your age or close to it, someone with the same values and with whom you can communicate on every level. Don't edit your thoughts, feelings, and values to please someone else; express them as they truly are. This is really important and, alas, one of my great failings.

Great sex is, of course, a top priority. Over the long haul it comes and goes, goes and comes, but hang in there. Make every effort to remain faithful; it will make you happier than you already are.

Oh, and marry someone who makes you laugh. This is perhaps most important of all.

As for other regrets? I regret the times I said no when the answer should have been yes, and vice versa.

I regret the years of separation between my mother and me, and that when we did reconcile, we never, ever discussed what had happened between us.

I now understand that I was far more related in spirit to

Auntie Ger than to my mother, but Auntie Ger and I never
became close enough to be aware of this. Another regret.

I regret the few times I hurt Sidney Lumet, though I am
relieved he knew of the great love I had for him and still do.
Most of all, I regret tearing up without reading the letter
from Catholic Charities advising me that Dodo was on her
deathbed, and that I was not by her side when she died.

Although I tend to be hard on myself and don't often feel I
am qualified to give advice, there is one thing I do believe in
above all else: love.

Love Is All.

Despite all that has happened to me, or perhaps because of
it, of this I am certain. Can one ever love too much? Trust too
much? Not in my book. Love and trust are my truths. They
rarely fail, except when I don't listen to my instincts.

I believe even now that a great love, a true love, is seeking
me out as I am seeking him. Until you find that person, you
will rush down many paths leading nowhere. These are
tests from which you can learn truths about yourself and
discover who you really are. There will be many Prince
Charmings who turn into toads before the one you seek
appears.

When you do finally meet your love, honestly confide in
him. Hold nothing back. Not only the high hopes you have,

but also the dark fear that you may not be capable of taking responsibility for another person's happiness.

Show each other that you not only love but also respect each other. Define your values, but know that you both must be willing to compromise. Believe that the life you create together is the top priority and you will do all you can to make it work.

I recently came across a saying by the Scottish writer Ian Maclaren. "Be kind," he wrote, "for everyone you meet is fighting a great battle."

You may not be able to see the battle others are fighting, and you may believe they are confident and have never known sadness or fear, but believe me, they have, so be kind.

Take heed,

Gloria

S omeone recently said to me that it is easier to be clever than it is to be kind, and I think that is very true. So I add to my list of regrets the times I have not been kind, choosing instead to be clever, usually at someone else's expense.

We began this conversation the day you turned ninety-one. You are now a few months shy of ninety-two. As a reporter, I try never to ask that stupid question "How does it feel," but has your vantage point changed a lot?

After a lot of living, I have become the mother and father I never had, like one of those Russian wooden dolls you open to find a smaller doll inside, and then another inside that, until you come to the smallest doll of all: yourself.

Age begins to dawn on us only as we grow older. It's in the shadow we cast on the pavement one sunny day. It's in the image reflected in a glass window on a busy street as we pass by.

Who is that?

Could it be the girl who, as a child, craved to be grown up, to be old, which meant to be independent and in control? From the time I was eleven until I was sixteen, the days, from dawn to dusk, crept along seemingly without end. How I wanted to be free to leap up onto that rainbow so far, far out of reach.

Of course, Andy, I must appear to you to be not only very old, but ancient. I assure you, that is not how I appear to myself. No doubt, you will believe me to be in denial, but this is not so.

How does it look from this high up on the bridge? Pretty good, actually. No impulse to jump into the river below as it winds "somewhere safe to sea" as Swinburne wrote—just curiosity about what's going to happen next. Unexpected gifts await as age takes hold; past tragedies, although never forgotten, are made more bearable, settling into a landscape that is mercifully behind me.

The low self-esteem, the insecurities I've harbored since childhood are largely resolved. I trust myself. I have energy. I remain active. Last year I had three exhibits of my paintings. I have close family and devoted friends, a passionate love of beauty, and I still believe in romance, lovely things can happen when you least expect them. . . . The phone can ring, and your whole life can change in a blink (for better, of course!).

All this may sound like pie in the sky, but why not? Isn't pie in the sky (my choice being angel lemon meringue) more soothing, not to mention more energizing, and conducive to pressing on than, say, a rose rooted in the earth with its blossoms drooping to the ground eventually dying for lack of water?

Oh hell, please don't label me a hopeless optimist. We all have moments when we die a little, or a lot. But stay calm. Take a look at yourself in the mirror. No crying, please. These moments can be the beginning of a rebirth, another chance to reinvent yourself.

"The rainbow comes and goes," Wordsworth wrote, and boy, was he right.

T he rainbow comes and goes."
    I like the slight note of resignation that phrase implies—the acceptance that things can't always be good.

The rainbow does come and go for all of us, but what is

remarkable about you is that you still believe it is out there even when you can't see it, and you keep moving forward, searching for it, even on the darkest of days. That is what you have always done. You believe the rainbow will always return and that, around the corner, a new adventure waits: a man with a boat who might whisk you off to the South of France; a creative project that might become a big business.

As you know, I am more of a realist, perhaps even a catastrophist. I prefer both those words to *pessimist*. I plan and prepare always for the worst-case scenario.

You are certainly not a hopeless optimist, and I am always rather skeptical of those who are, but you are relentless in your determination to find the rainbow, and because of that, you remain one of the most modern people I know.

I find it reassuring knowing the rainbow comes and goes. It helps me accept the way things often are.

In every life, you have moments of blinding beauty and happiness, and then you land in a dark cave and there is no color, no sky. Then the rainbow returns, sometimes only briefly, but it always does come back. You have to believe that it will, even in the darkest of times. That belief is what is really important.

Nothing is meant to last forever. Our lives are fleeting. We surround ourselves with objects, collect things, try to hold on to people and money and status, but it doesn't last.

We are not meant always to be happy, and who would want to be? Happiness would become meaningless if it were a constant state. If you accept that, then you will not be surprised when something bad occurs, you will not gnash your teeth and ask, "Why me? Why has this happened to me?"

It has happened to you because that is the nature of things. No one escapes.

The rainbow comes and goes. Enjoy it while it lasts. Don't be surprised by its departure, and rejoice when it returns.

There is so much to be joyful about, so many different kinds of rainbows in one's life: making love is an incredible rainbow, as is falling in love; knowing friendship; being able to really talk with someone who has a problem and say something that will help; waking up in the morning, looking out, and seeing a tree that has suddenly blossomed, like the one I have outside my window—what joy that brings. It may seem a small thing, but rainbows come in all sizes.

I think about Dorothy in *The Wizard of Oz* singing, about where "bluebirds fly," and Jan Peerce singing about "a bluebird of happiness." Well, they may never find it, they may never reach it, and that's okay. The searching, that's what I think life is really all about. Don't you?

I'm not sure I believe in always searching for it. I know the rainbow will come back. It always does in nature, but how can you be sure you will be there when it appears? I would much rather teach myself to be comfortable in the darkness, save money, buy supplies, prepare for the long winter. If a rainbow breaks out—well then, what a lovely surprise!

I do wish I had a little more of your hopefulness. I used to think that because I've spent so much time over the past twenty years working in war zones and disaster areas that my caution was born of experience, but I don't think it is just that. I was cautious long before I ever thought of becoming a reporter.

So much of my current outlook has been shaped by early loss. I know yours was as well, yet each of us has reacted differently to those losses. I became far more independent, and began teaching myself that I could survive on my own no matter what, proving to myself that even if the rainbow didn't come back, I would be just fine.

I think your way makes much more sense. I'm certainly not advocating my way for others. Had I been more of a realist, perhaps I would have avoided many of the dreadful mistakes I made in my life and not trusted people I shouldn't have.

As I've said, I am not an optimist, but it is in my nature to be hopeful; there is a huge difference between the two. It's some sort of a gene I was born with, and though it has not always served me well, I would not want to be any other way. I think I have a lot more fun because I am open to new experiences, and it doesn't always turn out badly.

The advantage of being trusting is you don't harden, which I admire. I don't like hard people. By remaining open, you live in a way that's more productive.

The risk is that you can lose everything, and I have at times, or nearly everything.

I remember Dodo once said to me, "You don't know the world, Gloria."

I wasn't sure what she was talking about, and I wish now I had pursued the conversation.

Anderson, because of your experiences in the world of journalism, your worldview is far more encompassing than mine. You are far more wary and suspicious than I could ever be. But you have not made the mistake of hardening your heart, despite all that you have seen. You have not lost one shred of humanity, integrity, or compassion.

Although we come from very different starting points, the end result, the openness to others and ideas, is the same. It is in my nature to trust with an open heart, my gut instinct the only compass I follow. At times it is right on the mark; at other times, far off it.

I do now know the world, the good and the bad, and I would

rather greet it with open arms; it is worth the hurt, the sting of loss or betrayal. Yes, worth it all.

Hope is essential. The alternative is to stop living.

It never occurs to me that the rainbow will not come back. As you said, I just know there is a yacht, or at least a big rowboat, waiting for me in the Mediterranean right now, and someday I'm going to be on it with all my loved ones. You're invited, of course. You can make things happen by willing it. It's like praying. Hope has energy and its own life force to make dreams come true.

I wish I shared your belief. I pray every night for those I care about and worry about, but I don't believe you can make things happen just by willing them to. I've seen a lot of people who really wanted something good to happen in their lives, and it didn't. The world is full of people with dashed hopes, living in unfair circumstances, good people who deserve a better hand than the one they've been dealt. It's not a lack of will that prevents them from changing their lives. I'm all for believing in the power of will, but only if it spurs me to work harder.

It's not that I don't have dreams, hopes, and ambitions, but I would rather work to achieve them, and if I can't, I want to be at peace with that.

I don't want to envision a yacht somewhere out there waiting for me. I don't want to dream of something that doesn't come to pass. It may sound dull and unimaginative of me, but I don't want to be disappointed if it never materializes. I would much rather be present in the reality of now, learn to accept what is, not what might be someday.

I still feel my life and career are on the upswing. I am still learning new things, still getting better at my job. But I worry about the day I no longer have that feeling, when the best of everything is past and I am in decline. It is inevitable of course; that day will come, and sooner than I can imagine. I just hope I can handle it with grace.

Andy, the longer you live, the more brilliantly you will soar. The sky is the limit for you in whatever pursuits you choose; of this I am certain. No need to fear "inevitable decline." My career didn't really start taking off big time until I launched Gloria Vanderbilt jeans. I was fifty-four. Listen to your Mamacita: you have time, lots and lots of time.

I appreciate the positivity, but I usually discount positive things. It may not be a healthy habit, but I worry always about becoming complacent.

When I went to Hanoi after college to study Vietnamese, I learned that some Vietnamese people believe that if a baby is very pretty you never say, "Oh my, what a pretty baby."

You say, instead, "That is an ugly baby. How can a baby be so ugly?"

You do this so evil spirits in the air don't hear that there is a beautiful baby and take him away. This is one of the few superstitions I pay attention to and have expanded to cover more than just babies. I tend to avoid saying anything too positive about myself or my circumstances. Why tempt any evil spirits that might be floating around somewhere?

You telling me, "The sky is the limit," makes me want to search for some wood to knock on. As you know better than anyone, the sky can fall at any moment, and I want to be ready when it does. I don't want to be one of those people who find themselves lost when they are no longer valued at their job, or passed over by someone younger and smarter. I want to be ready for what is to come, the good and the bad.

Well, I understand the fear, which is natural, but as your mom, I am allowed to imagine accelerating and infinite heights for you. That is what mothers do. Excelsior!

I just received today a letter from my old school chum Prudence Gayheart, whose counsel applies more to you than it does to me. This is what she wrote:

Stop this dwelling on fantasy tragedies and disasters occurring unexpectedly. It is time wasted and leads to a dead end; such pursuits sap and waste energy. You tend to worry much too much over bad things occurring, events that may never happen. You can do this if you put your mind to it. Whenever those thoughts pop up, just give them a swift kick in the ass.

She always did have a way with words, even way back when we were in high school.

Take her words to heart. Let them sink in. Please. Of course what you must come to terms with, what we all must define, is what success means for each of us. Money, fame, praise from co-workers, career advancement? Are these your definitions of success? They are for many people. But I believe there are many kinds of success: happiness with one's work, the feeling that you are making an important contribution, helping people in one way or another, creating something that speaks to you or to others, loving someone who loves you, creating honest relationships, giving of yourself to someone and getting something back.

It is very easy simply to define yourself by your job, your title, your salary, but these rarely give you long-term feelings of success and happiness.

Your father was a fine writer, but he never sold a huge number of books or reached the level of renown that was his dream. But he knew that his greatest success, his most important achievement, was you and Carter, creating you, and raising you, teaching you and talking with you. That is what he lived for and tried to stave off death for.

All these other benchmarks by which people define success: money, power, fame, Instagram likes, followers on Twitter— they are all meaningless. They aren't real. Money can give you independence, but once you start chasing it, there will never be enough. No amount will make you feel whole or safe.

The problem arises when no matter how successful you become, the rainbow is still not enough. When you think it could always be brighter, and last longer.

I know this for a fact. Yes, you can buy beautiful things, and live in a nice home, and provide for those you love. That is certainly important, and it has been important to me, but it doesn't last, and it doesn't take away the feelings of loss and pain that exist in one's core.

Anderson, you have a loving partner, a fascinating career, and independence. Who could be more blessed?

I think of my own life and the circles that it has taken. It's so amazing to me that I went to live at 10 Gracie Square in New York when I was married to Leopold Stokowski, and then I moved, and then, decades later, quite by chance, lived there again with you and Carter. Now I live in a building your father once lived in long ago. No one knows what lies ahead.

Go to the top of the Empire State Building. Gaze down as far as the eye can see, way down onto the streets below. People by the thousands, each going to their destiny on the streets of New York, each related to you and to me in some way, some aware of this, others not, or not yet.

A woman in a red jacket turns the corner. Later today, she may be dead. This is the battle. No one escapes. So be kind.

I want to write one final letter before we turn the corner on this conversation we've been having. Early on you remarked that we both shared the fantasy that a letter from our fathers might one day arrive.

It's not the same, but I thought I would write you a letter that you can read from time to time after I have departed. Keep it somewhere in a box, knowing that when you are reading it, I am close by, closer even than you think. It is not the same kind of letter we both imagined, but I hope it is something that will remind you of me and the love I have for you.

Darling Anderson,

I need not try to find words to express how proud I am of what you have made and are making of your life. And Daddy—WOW. But he always knew it would happen this way. Watching him with you and Carter, seeing the father he was and is to you, was a revelation to me. He showed me what it meant for a child to have a parent.

Wyatt Cooper was the most honest person I met in my life. That honesty reflected his intent in the way he lived his life, his values, and what he hoped for the family he created when he married me.

I not only sense, I know, these values reside in you. I fervently hope that you will become a father. If this is to be, don't wait too long. When Wyatt and I were talking about getting married, I had what I considered chic streaks of gray in my hair.

"I want us to be young parents," he said. Immediately I took the hint and started coloring my hair.

You have already achieved so much in your life that it would be hard to imagine that you could ever doubt yourself. And you did it on your own.

But I understand and know too well that no matter what one achieves, it is never enough. Whenever this restlessness, this lack of contentment hits, remember what Billy Wilder said to Jack Lemmon: "You're as good as the best thing you've ever done."

Anderson, in your case, that's pretty damn good.

As for your mom—she's failed so often, in so many ways, struggling to keep afloat in dark seas growing up. I only hope that you will try to understand and, in doing so, forgive in any way I may have failed you. It was certainly not my intent. It is good to know at this point in my life that you have become as close to me as you are to Daddy, and that makes up for all the times I failed.

Success and the money it brings are a great high, but the greatest high of all and the most difficult to achieve is a happy family life. Consider making a loving partner and a family your true foundation of success. Please give it serious thought. Who knows, I hope I'll still be around if it happens.

If not, please keep a photograph of me somewhere nearby for your son or daughter to glance at now and then. Only tell them the good things about me, how much I loved you, the happy times we had together as a family. And that someday, they'll grow up, and if they choose, make a family of their own, and be happy, too.

We are told the fable ends with a pot of gold at the end of the rainbow. But does it? I have no answer, except to say, I know the rainbow comes and goes, and really, isn't that enough?

Your Adoring Mom

Epilogue

As my mom's ninety-second birthday approached, we decided to conclude this conversation we had begun one year before. But a conversation like this never really ends once it has started. In the weeks since, we have spoken often and with a level of understanding that is deeper and truer than ever. Something fundamental changed between us this past year. I think of my mother differently, and I know she feels the same.

When I remember all those I have lost in my life, I think of all the questions I wish I had asked them, the things I wish I had told them. I will have no such regrets with my mom, and for that I am very thankful.

The other day she sent me the following e-mail:

Willa Cather wrote, "The heart of another is a dark forest, always no matter how close to one's own."

How close have our hearts come together in these pages?

ANDERSON COOPER and
Gloria Vanderbilt

*If nothing else, it can be said: Closer than before as light
shines through.*

I'm not quite sure what that last line means, but I like the
way it sounds, and it has stuck in my head.

When I called her to see what she wanted to do for her
ninety-second birthday, she told me she didn't want to celebrate the occasion. At first I found this sad, but then I realized she no longer has any need to celebrate just one single
day of the year. At ninety-two, each day is a kind of celebration, a chance to read a new book, begin a new painting, or
simply reflect on all she's lived through. When she wakes up,
she takes a moment to make a wish, then gets out of bed and
makes it come true.

The day of her birthday, I picked her up from her apartment and we did something we have not done together for
quite a while, but something we often did in the past, in good
times and bad.

We went to see a movie.

As I mentioned previously, after my father died, she and I
used to go see movies together a lot. It was a way for us to be
together and yet also forget for a few hours the sadness we
felt.

As I grew older and got busier with school we saw movies
together less and less, but after my brother killed himself

we were faced with the dilemma of oncoming holidays and how we would get through them. Neither of us wanted to observe Thanksgiving or Christmas, or any other kind of day requiring a celebration. When you are grieving, the holidays, with their cards and constant commercials, remind you of the holes in your heart and all that you have lost.

So after my brother's death, we once again returned to the movies, and that is how we got through holidays for several years. No tree on Christmas, no turkey on Thanksgiving, no exchange of presents—just the other's company in a darkened theater waiting to be transported for a few hours to another world.

This trip to the movies on my mother's ninety-second birthday was different, however. As we sat sharing some popcorn and chatting before the film began, I realized we were not avoiding a painful holiday; we were celebrating together all that we had been through.

During the film, I occasionally glanced over and saw her not just as a woman of ninety-two, but as a girl of thirteen watching a movie with Tootsie Eleanor, dreaming of what her adult life would one day be like.

I remembered that I had sat with her in that same theater when I was thirteen and we were still getting to know each other after my father's sudden death, and it was the same theater we had come to the first Christmas after my brother died, both trying to imagine how we would get through the day.

After the movie ended, we headed slowly back to her apartment. We spoke a little about the film, but much of the way was spent in silence, walking down the street arm in arm. There was no need to talk.

I know her. She knows me.

She is my mother. I am her son.

The rainbow comes and goes.

Grateful acknowledgment is made for permission to reproduce images on the following pages:

Frontispiece: Photo by George Hoyningen-Huene, courtesy of R. J. Horst/Staley Wise Gallery.

Page 60: Photo by Keystone-France/Gamma-Keystone via Getty Images.

Page 71: The Harry Ransom Center, The University of Texas at Austin.

Page 125: Photo by Horst P. Horst/Conde Nast.

Page 142: Photo © Bettmann/CORBIS.

Page 162: AP Photo.

Page 168: AP Photo/Anthony Camerano.

All other images are courtesy of the authors.

About the Authors

ANDERSON COOPER is the anchor of *Anderson Cooper 360°* on CNN and a correspondent for CBS's *60 Minutes*. He has won numerous journalism awards and nine Emmys, and his first book, *Dispatches from the Edge*, was a number one *New York Times* bestseller. He lives in New York City.

GLORIA VANDERBILT is an American artist, writer, and designer. Her artwork can be found at GloriaVanderbiltfineart.com. She is the author of eight books and has been a regular contributor to the *New York Times*, *Vanity Fair*, and *Elle*. She lives in New York City.